A Peoples Education Skillbook for

AP*/Honors

Entering the Conversation

Key Skill Elements for Successful Academic
Writing in AP* Language and Literature

By Stephen Heller
and Steven Fox

Peoples Education®
Your partner in student success®

About the Authors

Stephen Heller

Stephen Heller (Ph.D., Loyola University of Chicago) teaches AP English Language and Composition, College Prep Junior English, and Freshman Accelerated English at Adlai E. Stevenson High School in Lincolnshire, Illinois, where he has been on the faculty since 1999. A teacher for 23 years, Steve has served as a question leader, table leader, and reader for the AP English Language and Composition exam. He is also a College Board consultant for Pre-AP/English Vertical Teams and AP English Language and Composition.

From 1987 to 2008, Steve taught at Northwestern University's Center for Talent Development, where he worked with students in accelerated language arts classes. Prior to working at Adlai E. Stevenson High School, Steve taught at Oak Lawn Community High School, Glenbard East High School, and Morgan Park Academy—all in the Chicagoland area. For the last five years he has co-taught American Themes in the AP Classroom, an interdisciplinary course that focuses upon skills common to AP English Language and Composition and AP U.S. History. Steve is also the coauthor of Peoples Education's *AP English Bound*.

Steve earned his Masters degree in English Education at the University of Illinois at Chicago, with David Jolliffe as his adviser, and earned his B.A. in English from Northwestern University in 1986. His writings have appeared in *English Journal* and the *Illinois Bulletin of English*. In 2005, he served as editor-in-chief of the College Board's Special Focus edition on Using Sources. Steve was a lead contributor to the authoring of the revised 2009 College Board workshop Pre-AP Strategies for English Vertical Teams. In 2006, the U.S. Department of Education awarded him the Teacher Recognition Award as part of the U.S. Presidential Scholars Program.

Steven Fox

Steven Fox taught for more than 30 years at Shaker Heights (Ohio) High School. After many years of teaching AP English Literature and Composition, he proposed and then designed and taught his school's AP English Language and Composition program. He has been a reader and table leader at both the English Literature and English Language AP exam readings for many years. Steven has been an essay reader for several other national examination programs and a test item writer for the ACT. He is currently a diploma examiner for the International Baccalaureate Program.

As an endorsed consultant, National Leader, and consultant mentor for the College Board, Steven provides workshops and summer institutes for both AP English courses and many pre-AP programs as well. He also works as a writer and staff developer for the AVID Center of San Diego. For the College Board, he wrote The *Official SAT Study Guide* in preparation for the revised SAT, and the accompanying *Teachers' Guide*. He provided additional materials for the high school edition of Andrea Lunsford's *Easy Writer*. He is the author of Peoples Education's *Advanced Composition Skills: 20 Lessons for AP Success* and a coauthor of *AP English Bound*.

In 1988, the Ohio Council of Teachers of English Language Arts chose Steven as Ohio's Outstanding English Language Arts Instructor of the year. In that same year he was awarded a Fulbright Teacher Exchange, and spent the 1988–1989 school year teaching at the Charles Read Secondary Modern School in Corby Glen, Lincolnshire, England.

Editorial and Project Manager: David Nazarian

Director of Permissions: Kristine Liebman

Editorial/Permissions Research: Amy Priddy Wierzbicki

Editorial Development: Publishing Solutions Group

Design and Production: Publishing Solutions Group

Cover: Tracy Clarry

*AP is a registered trademark of the College Board, which was not involved in the production of, and does not endorse, this book.

ISBN 978-1-936029-44-0

Copyright © 2011
Peoples Education, Inc.
299 Market Street
Saddle Brook, New Jersey 07663

Manufactured in Newburyport, MA in September 2010 by BRADFORD & BIGELOW, INC.
Printed in the United States of America.
10 9 8 7 6 5 4 3 2 1

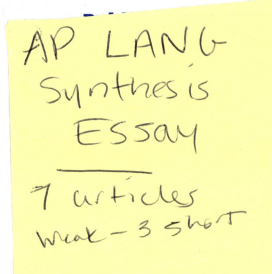

ledgements

...ledges the following AP/Honors English teachers and
...t materials during preparation for publication.

...School

...High School

...strict

...chool

...School

...Cactus Shadows High School

Valerie Schulman – Chichester School District

Alice Stephens – Oldenburg Academy of the Immaculate Conception

Suzanne Wexler – White Station High School

Contents

Guide to the Table of Contents

Unit titles *convey six distinct academic discourse communities that encompass the literary and rhetorical domains of English Language and Literature.*

Portals *convey a method of entry into the text—as both a reader and a writer. These portals represent commonly practiced methods of entry into text, but they are by no means an exhaustive list.*

Units 1–3 *feature portals that address those discourse communities of* **AP English Language and Composition**. *These are rhetorical analysis, argument, and synthesis. Further, these chapters are arranged sequentially, so that skills in analytical work inform skills in argumentation, which, in turn, culminate in more sophisticated work with synthesis.*

Units 4–6 *feature portals that address those discourse communities of* **AP English Literature and Composition**. *These are poetry analysis, prose analysis, and the open-ended response. Like the first three units, these units are arranged sequentially, so that analytical skills inform the open-ended question. Furthermore, the skills developed in Units 1–3 also inform the skills of Units 4–6, particularly as skills in argumentation and synthesis appear in Units 4–6.*

Unit 1: Rhetorical Analysis

This unit features analysis of rhetoric, with attention to public discourse, such as political speech, and private discourse, such as memoir. This unit also features evaluation of an argument, whereby analysis of rhetoric is accompanied by an informed evaluation on the cogency of the position.

Unit 2: Argument

This unit features modes of argumentation, with primary attention to the classical model—where students agree with, disagree with, or qualify a position—and the Rogerian model—where students look for points of truth throughout the argument. This unit also features comparison of competing arguments as a precursor to the chapter on synthesis.

Unit 3: Synthesis

This unit features the two major modes of using sources to formulate an original argument: the argumentative synthesis, which asks students to agree with, disagree with, or qualify a position; and the explanatory synthesis, which asks students to determine what factors or concepts need to be considered prior to making an informed judgment.

Unit 4: Poetry Analysis

This unit features distinct modes of analyzing poetry. First is the analysis of a poem's purpose or theme, with focus on poetic devices. Second is the analysis of a poem with attention to its rhetoric or argument. Third is the comparison of poems as they present distinct methods by which to communicate a central idea.

Unit 5: Prose Analysis

This unit features distinct modes of analyzing prose. First is the analysis of persona, where students focus as much on the speaker as they do the subject. Second is the analysis of prose techniques as the driving agent in the service of a given theme. The third portal looks at the theme or purpose as the driving agent of analysis.

Unit 6: The Open-Ended Response

This unit features distinct methods of responding to the open-ended response, each of which features literary argument. The first treats the text chronologically in the service of a given theme; the second approaches the text with an eye towards the use and effect of an element.

To the Teacher

English teachers spend a great deal of their time providing commentary on their students' writing. Ideally, students take these comments for their instructional value, and over the years of our careers, we teachers develop approaches to assessing our students' papers that we think will help them develop their writing skills the most.

We would not suggest that one textbook can include all the kinds of observations that a teacher might make about his or her students' writing. However, we do believe that among the most productive approaches is one that encourages students to become familiar with the discourse community that exists in relation to the essay the student is writing, and to enter into a conversation with those who have spoken before. In other words, our students are not the first to write literary analysis or original argument; they are not even the first to analyze "The Road Not Taken" or to express a position on whether or not the school should adopt or abolish a dress code. Just as writers discussing some significant world-wide issue, such as immigration reform, would not be successful if they did not put their comments into the context of what their audience already knows on the subject, our students need to write with an awareness of how writers before them have handled their expressions on the topics at hand. In short, they need to enter an existing conversation, rarely to begin one.

To that end we are presenting six discourse communities into which our students are often invited to enter: rhetorical analysis, synthesis, argument, prose analysis, poetry analysis, and open-ended commentary on literature. In each case, students will find that there are certain entry points—we are calling them portals—through which they will find easy access to the community of thinkers and writers they are seeking to join. Once inside the portal, the student will encounter a series of templates that represent the kind of thinking that typically takes place when one engages in the kind of discourse under discussion. Familiarity with these templates and thoughtful use of them should help the student craft an essay that addresses and develops its topic with a good measure of substance and focus. The templates act like training wheels. It should not take long before the students feel that they can balance on their own and ride off down the road gracefully. They will know what their readers need to see, and they will have the skills to provide it.

Each portal represents a familiar entry point in response to a writing prompt, and each prompt is accompanied by a sample response that makes use of the templates. These responses are provided with analysis of both the writer's response to the prompt (seeing how the writer actually answered the question) and the use of templates to facilitate that response.

We believe that to be a good writer one must also be a regular and observant reader. Successful writing does not exist in a vacuum. So we encourage students to read, to observe how authors of fiction or nonfiction advance the topics they are exploring, and then themselves to enter into the conversation with confidence.

Stephen Heller
Steven Fox

AP* English Bound and Entering the Conversation

The same authors' *AP* English Bound,* also published by Peoples Education, provides a unique opportunity for vertical articulation with *Entering the Conversation.*

AP English Bound,* like *Entering the Conversation,* articulates the relationship between the literary and rhetorical aspects of the English classroom, though the former addresses the pre-AP level, while the latter addresses the AP level.

For example, in lesson 9 of *AP* English Bound,* students are introduced to the task of synthesis, or combining sources, in the service of a larger argument. By experiencing this task at the pre-AP level, students will be better prepared to enter into this discourse community—chapter 3 of *Entering the Conversation*—at the actual AP level.

Further, the writing objectives of *AP* English Bound* identify those foundational skills common to all writing assignments—whether the assignments are more literary or rhetorical in nature. The skills developed are the building blocks.

Entering the Conversation, by comparison, takes those building blocks in writing and extends them into the six distinct discourse communities that students will enter in either AP course.

But *Entering the Conversation* goes further, providing an actual vocabulary for students to enter into these conversations. This vocabulary is best regarded in terms of the use of **templates**, tried and true statements that mark an awareness of and a willingness to **participate** in an accepted mode of discourse. These templates also serve as navigational elements by which students may more effectively move through their text.

Indeed, a second bridge between *AP* English Bound* and *Entering the Conversation* focuses on the use of portals, or entry points by which students will read and understand text. If in *AP* English Bound* we offer two distinct lenses through which to view text, in *Entering the Conversation* we offer closer to sixteen, for each discourse community carries with it a set of portals, or entry points, that monitor the ways in which a text can be understood.

Also available to teachers:

"Continuing the Conversation" Supplement
These materials provide additional prompts that allow students to further apply their learning. These prompts illustrate the objectives of each portal within each discourse community and cover the range of discourse communities found in either AP English course.

Teacher Guide for *Entering the Conversation*
These materials provide sample responses to the exercises and prompts presented in *Entering the Conversation*, and suggested strategies for how best to integrate *Entering the Conversation* into your instructional practice.

To the Student

Speaking and Writing

Chances are, most of what we say is in response to what we have heard.

Parents make "requests," aunts and uncles pay us compliments, friends ask for help. It is fairly easy to reply to any of these: what they want from us is fairly clear, and all we have to do is speak up and answer them. Sometimes, we might want to speak up even when we aren't the ones being spoken to. We might happen upon a conversation in which we overhear a proposal we could support from our own experience, a fact we know is wrong or only partially right, or an idea that is being dismissed, but deserves to be taken seriously. We still have something to say, but it is hard to know how to jump in with just the right words.

Having the right words is not always easy. In the first set of examples, we probably could speak up fairly easily because we've had experience before, and we know what works best to calm down Dad, or thank Aunt Martha, or tell Frankie from bio lab that he needs to start taking his own notes. But with the second set of examples, we need to introduce ourselves by how we say what we say. We need to sound intelligent but not pretentious, articulate but not wordy, informed but not overbearing. To say what we want to, we probably will draw from different sources—what we've read and what we've heard—in addition to paying attention to the dynamics of the conversation that we want to enter.

In a way, writing is a lot like speaking. We write in response to what we've read or heard. We reply to texts or emails, perhaps write editorials to the school newspaper in response to a notice on a bulletin board regarding cell phone use, or fill out applications for scholarships, summer programs, jobs, or college admission. For all of these, we need the right words, but, as we know from our conversations, different forms of writing require different vocabularies. The vocabulary that we choose to complete an application is going to be more formal than the shorthand we peck into a cell phone to text our friends about what we're doing.

The most formal vocabulary is probably that which we use for papers, responses to poems, stories, essays, and novels. When we respond to assignments such as these, we are entering a long-standing conversation; we are becoming part of a tradition, a tradition of serious readers and writers who want to express themselves about books and ideas that are important to them. These formal and established traditions of writing—often referred to as **discourse**—are those often taught and evaluated in high school and college, and they are used in much of the professional world later on.

Discourse Communities

The people who speak and write within a particular discourse are known as a **discourse community**. If you hear sportscasters on television, for example, talking about a game, you realize that they have a particular way of using language that seems appropriate to their subject matter and situation. They may have certain stock expressions and vocabulary that make their discourse sound knowledgeable and important. The same can be said about political commentators, or movie reviewers, or fashion analysts. If you want to sound as though you are up to date in any of those areas, you are likely to adopt some of their language characteristics. In other words, you try to join their discourse community.

The same is true of writing about literature or about the public interest topics that comprise the bulk of your written assignments in your English classes, as well as social studies, the sciences, and other academic departments. Your writing will sound more effective—probably more knowledgeable and more thorough—if it sounds like the writing of those who have established the characteristics of academic discourse. This book will help you develop techniques for sounding like a member of that community.

Writing and Templates

Just as the most sophisticated conversations can be the hardest to enter, so entering the conversation of academic discourse can seem intimidating at first. Sometimes, in high-level conversations, it is wise to listen for a few minutes, get a sense of how people are expressing themselves, and then proceed, using key terms and phrases that you have heard. Much in the way you learn to speak by imitating the language of those around you, so, too, can you internalize a language that is appropriate for an academic discourse.

Take, for example, a writing task that asks you to analyze the rhetoric of a candidate's speech. Part of this task requires you to understand the candidate's position. How do you state this in a way that is *understood* and *accepted* by readers who are already familiar with this task and know what to expect?

This book will teach you how to use *templates* to help you enter this and other writing conversations. You might have seen templates if you have ever worked with sheet metal, carpentry, or sewing. In those contexts, templates are preexisting models, usually made out of thin pieces of metal or wood, around which you cut the material that you have to get the shape that you want. In writing, a template is a preexisting model that you use to shape your sentences, depending upon the writing task that you have. In doing so, a template gives you language to imitate when you want to enter the conversation of written discourse. Templates such as the ones given below give you the language to imitate when you want to write about a candidate's speech:

> *The text's overall message or purpose is _____.*
> *The speaker understands that _____ is at stake.*

As you begin writing your response, you determine which template best suits your purpose and style. You may begin your response with this:

> *The candidate's overall purpose is to _____*

and in the blank, you state what you have determined the purpose to be. While you may be worried that when using a template someone else is dictating your language, rest assured that you have *complete freedom* to move away from it, once you are ready to speak confidently and clearly. To use a template effectively, you need to be a careful reader and a thoughtful writer. Just as the artisan needs rich material to use in creating a design, you too need rich material—quotations, examples, thoughts and ideas—to use a template effectively. In the above example, what is more important than the actual words is that you have a statement that clearly articulates what the candidate's purpose is. To use a template, you have to have something to say.

Lesson Guide

Unit 1

Rhetorical Analysis

Portal 1

Finding the Portal

Top-Down Analysis

How you respond to matters of public concern often depends on the manner in which those matters are presented to you. Be it a general rallying his troops, an advocate pleading for her cause, a disenfranchised member seeking passage of a bill—all of these messages attempt to appeal to you through emotion or logic.

How you enter a conversation with the speaker of those concerns—either through an oral or written response—depends upon your ability to analyze the speaker's rhetoric, for through such analysis you demonstrate your understanding of what's being said and how it's being said. The **top-down analysis** most closely replicates the role of listener, one whose primary obligation is to follow the text (or speech) from beginning to end.

Political speeches—or texts with a timely, topical intent to persuade—present a greater emphasis on the bottom half of Aristotle's rhetorical triangle, as seen here:

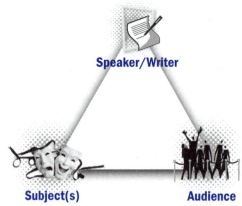

The Speaker/Writer strives to connect the Audience to the Subject(s).

Finding the Portal
This section reveals portals, or points of entry, into a given discourse community. Each unit in this textbook provides 2 or 3 common portals for each discourse community.

The Reading Experience

This section introduces the portal through the eyes and ears of a reader, and it illustrates common features of the reading experience necessary to write effectively.

The Writing Experience

This section provides a general overview of what writers within this discourse community should consider as they enter into a written conversation.

Portal Points

Portal points highlight the key features readers and writers must remember to enter the discourse community.

The Reading Experience

Political speeches invite a "top-down" rhetorical analysis, whereby the reader starts at the top or beginning of the speech and works his or her way down, noting distinctive moves that the speaker (or writer) makes, and thereby emulates the experience of the audience.

The top-down analysis of rhetoric approaches the text from the beginning to the end. It is more than just a play-by-play analysis, however, as you must first have a sense of the overall purpose of the text. That purpose relates to the basic point or **message** that the author wants to convey. That purpose may be to warn of an impending danger, argue for the passage of certain laws or policies, or commemorate key events in the past or present, but behind good formal writing or speaking there is an exigent purpose in delivering that message. In some cases, the text will reveal such a message more explicitly, but often there is a more implicit message that reveals itself through analysis.

The Writing Experience

The top-down analysis also calls for a more expansive approach toward understanding an author's purpose. As you analyze text from top to bottom, you will discover as your analysis evolves how the writer's purpose evolves. Your own analysis becomes a new lens through which to view the original text. At the heart of rhetorical analysis lie two questions: **What is the author's message?** and **How is this message being communicated?** In the same manner in which you read a text from top to bottom, so, too, can your analysis follow a similar direction.

PORTAL POINTS FOR WRITING TOP-DOWN ANALYSIS:

The top-down analysis allows you to write a play-by-play analysis of the text and put yourself squarely in the role of the audience. Key points to consider as you write a top-down analysis are:

- the overall message or purpose of the text;
- the ways in which the message evolves;
- the techniques the writer/speaker employs in the service of this evolution.

To help you write a top-down analysis, examine the following templates. Think of these templates not only as a road map of what direction to take in your writing, but also as useful vocabulary for this direction.

Writing Templates

These templates provide suggestions on how to enter and move through a conversation within a specific discourse community. Each portal has its own set of templates which provide analytical and rhetorical strategies as well as guides on how your writing can be a part of a written conversation.

Templates for Top-Down Rhetorical Analysis

▼ **Introducing the cause or exigence**
These templates introduce the writer's passion or reason for being.

The text's overall message or purpose is _____.

The speaker understands that _____ is at stake.

Within the context of _____, the writer argues for _____.

▼ **Acknowledging opposing views or concessions**
These templates introduce sensitivity for other sides and increase your own credibility.

By first acknowledging _____, the writer achieves _____.

Prior to arguing for _____, the speaker must first acknowledge _____.

The reason that the speaker begins with _____ is that _____.

It does seem paradoxical that the text would state _____, especially given _____.

The reasons that the writer argues for _____ become clear only when we reach the end of the text.

▼ **Refutations that build upon concession**
These templates allow you to thoughtfully balance all views with your own.

Once the opposite side has been recognized, the text can now more credibly address _____.

While the concession features a more conciliatory tone, the text shifts toward _____ in arguing for its point.

Now that the audience has been embraced through the concession, the writer can now make his main point that _____.

The writer achieves greater credibility by first conceding _____, which is then immediately followed with her main idea that _____.

While the concession relies more upon _____ [pick one: logic or emotion], the refutation works because it focuses the argument on [pick the other: logic or emotion].

Essay Prompts

Sample prompts illustrate how the written conversation that draws a writer into a discourse community begins. These AP-level writing prompts are designed to help you prepare for either AP English course.

Guided Practice

This section focuses on how to access a specific practice text first as a reader. Annotations reflect analysis of that text.

Guided Practice

The Conversation Begins

A standard prompt for an essay of rhetorical analysis often features these two tasks:

• **Determine** the author's position on a given topic

• **Analyze** the rhetorical techniques he or she uses to achieve that position.

Notice how both of these tasks appear in the following prompt.

> Determine Barack Obama's main message(s) in his November 4, 2008, General Election Victory Speech, and analyze the techniques he uses to communicate that message.

To help you compose a successful essay in response to the prompt, complete the following steps.

Step 1: *Reading the text*

Prior to writing about a text is the careful reading of that text. As you read the sample text, read also the accompanying annotations for an analysis of the rhetoric.

Excerpt from *Barack Obama's General Election Victory Speech November 4, 2008*

I was never the likeliest candidate for this office. We didn't start with much money or many endorsements. Our campaign was not hatched in the halls of Washington—it began in the backyards of Des Moines and the living rooms of Concord and the front porches of
5 Charleston.

It was built by working men and women who dug into what little savings they had to give five dollars and ten dollars and twenty dollars to this cause. It grew strength from the young people who rejected the myth of their generation's apathy; who left their homes and their
10 families for jobs that offered little pay and less sleep; from the not-so-young people who braved the bitter cold and scorching heat to knock on the doors of perfect strangers; from the millions of Americans who volunteered, and organized, and proved that more than two centuries later, a government of the people, by the people and for the people has
15 not perished from this Earth. This is your victory.

I know you didn't do this just to win an election and I know you didn't do it for me. You did it because you understand the enormity of the task that lies ahead. For even as we celebrate tonight, we know the challenges that tomorrow will bring are the greatest of our lifetime—

Rhetorical annotation

Concessions through the words **never** and **didn't** acknowledge the opposition to his candidacy and his underdog status.

Parallelism invokes different kinds of people and occupations.

The distinctive use of pronouns establishes the speaker's relationship directly with his audience. Note the movement toward we, or unity.

> **Pre-Writing Exercises**
> These exercises organize the reading experience into preliminary questions that will move the act of reading towards the act of writing. **Discourse questions** and **graphic organizers** allow you to compile much of the evidence for an effective essay.

Step 2: *Pre-writing*

Discourse Questions To help you begin writing about the text, answer the following questions:

1. What is the exigence or urgent concern of this text?

2. What is the writer's message or purpose, and how does this message evolve?

3. In what way(s) does the speaker embrace his opponents?

4. Where do we see appeals to pathos? ethos? logic?

5. What features of the text's organization enhance its effectiveness?

6. What elements of language—especially diction, syntax, and metaphor—enhance the overall message?

7. Where does the tone shift? From what to what?

8. Who is the audience, and how does awareness of this audience impact the overall speech?

Notice how the discourse questions develop from the two basic questions: What is the author's message? (Questions 1-2) and How is this message being communicated? (Questions 3 through 8). This latter set of questions asks you to consider rhetorical devices or moves that the author made to engage the listener more actively. At this point in your analysis, you are answering two related but different questions: (a) What rhetorical move is the writing making? And (b) What is the effect of that move?

Record your observations in a 3-column chart, represented below:

What the author is saying?	How the author is saying it?	What are the effects of the author's moves?

The actual response again *builds* upon the template:

> By first acknowledging his outsider status, Obama achieves greater credibility; he claims he was not the "likeliest of candidates"

And the final template used actually occurs *within* a paragraph.

Guided Practice

Step 4: *Application of templates*

You Try It Up until now, you have been a listener. Now it is your turn to enter the conversation. On a separate page, continue the analysis of the Obama speech by answering the prompt for this section. Return to your graphic organizer from Step 2 to assist you here. As you work your way down the text, determine the moves the writer is making and the effects of those moves on the writer's overall purpose. Then, look at the catalogue of templates for the top-down rhetorical analysis located on pages 3 and 4 to help you construct key sentences in your response.

Excerpt for Practice

It was built by working men and women who dug into what little savings they had to give five dollars and ten dollars and twenty dollars to this cause. It drew strength from the young people who rejected the myth of their generation's apathy; who left their homes and their
10 families for jobs that offered little pay and less sleep; from the not-so-young people who braved the bitter cold and scorching heat to knock on the doors of perfect strangers; from the millions of Americans who volunteered, and organized, and proved that more than two centuries later, a government of the people, by the people and for the people has
15 not perished from this Earth. This is your victory.

Write your response and compare it with the following:

> ***Continuation of sample response to Obama's Victory Speech prompt***
> The speech builds upon its belief in unity in the next paragraph, as Obama's parallelism lists supporters who encompass a range of Americans who braved dire conditions to support his candidacy. These conditions, listed as an accumulation of increasingly difficult circumstances, reinforce the image of an American who has less financial power. Obama's diction moves from objects of apathy and discomfort—money, bitter cold, strangers—and then returns to verbs of strength: volunteer, organize, prove. In so doing, Obama reveals the American spirit to revive itself under difficult times, and by ending the sentence with a reference to Lincoln's Gettysburg Address, the parallels of a nation divided and the potential for a government to solve this are drawn. On a larger scale, Obama is calling for unity, much as Lincoln did.

This template joins purpose and rhetorical technique.

This template joins technique and purpose.

Application of Templates
This section illustrates the use of templates, provides commentary on how the templates have been applied, and gives you additional practice in using the templates for the remainder of the sample essay.

Discovering Portals and Templates

Using templates

Whether you are writing a rhetorical or literary analysis, argument, or synthesis essay, you are entering into a type of conversation that many others have already entered. The challenge, of course, is to add your own original voice and contribution, and not just to conform to what others have already said about a given topic. Therefore, the balance becomes a tricky one: how do you enter into an already-established conversation, and at the same time provide your own individual voice?

Just like any other form of expression—dressing, singing, dancing—you model your work on acceptable and understandable modes of communication. On the one hand, good modeling requires curiosity and observation. Musicians listen attentively to the style and technique of other musicians to learn how to create certain effects. On the other hand, however, good modeling involves creativity and ideas of your own. A rock musician may study the techniques of classical composers to learn how to suggest mood or emotion, but use those techniques on different instruments or enhance them by using computer technology. Modeling is not simply copying.

How do I select a template?

Entering any kind of conversation, both spoken and written, is a bit like going on a journey. Through the exchange of ideas, participants, if they are good listeners and effective communicators, end up in a different place from where they were when the conversation began. Usually, in a written conversation, you know where that destination is, because you have a specific point to make, a particular idea that will become part of the larger conversation of ideas on a specific topic. Consider a template as a road map. If you are traveling from point A to point B and you need directions, the template provides not only moves or specific directions that you can take in your writing, but also the language you can use to take those directions. The key here is that you know what final destination you are headed towards; the template merely guides.

Consider, too, that there are often many ways to get to your destination. This is why a *menu* of templates exists, in order to give you the opportunity to determine the different paths you could choose to illuminate your ideas in this written conversation. As you are writing, you review that menu, explore what the purpose of each template is, and you also "listen" to its language; then, you insert it into your essay in the location of your choice. In this text, models are provided for you to "listen" to, as well as commentary that will help you learn how to insert templates strategically into your writing. Remember, however, that these are merely tools to help you to learn how to use the templates effectively on your own.

Templates can appear anywhere in your writing: as an introductory statement, a transitional device between paragraphs, a summative statement within a paragraph, and as a concluding observation over the entire work.

Remember, the templates do *not* do the writing for you; as with a map with *many* different routes, your task is to know which direction you plan to take.

How can I adapt a template?

Because your own voice remains central to any written conversation, it is crucial that you look at the template's *purpose* as much as its actual language. Modifying a template means more than just substituting, adding, or subtracting words from the template, though those are certainly good forms of adaptation. Perhaps one way to think of adaptation is to recall the first time you used a new word. It felt awkward, wooden, perhaps forced, perhaps uttered in an uncertain or unfamiliar tone. Yet the more you used that word, the more you came to understand its meaning. You learned how to use it subtly and thoughtfully, how to use it deliberately to make the point you wanted to make. So too with templates. The more you make use of a template, the more you internalize its meaning and, in time, artfully and skillfully adapt it to conform to your own needs as a thoughtful reader and writer.

The template will never be a substitute for your voice. Rather, it will be the means by which you can use that voice to connect with other thinkers and writers.

When should I incorporate a template?

There are two distinct times to consider incorporating a template. The first is when you are uncertain about what direction to take. You are in search of ways to argue a position, agree with, disagree with, or adapt someone else's ideas, or bring together a number of ideas or pieces of information. If you pull out the map of templates and look for some navigational tools, the template will tell you what rhetorical or analytical moves you can make and what they will sound like. The second is when you are more certain that you know the rhetorical or analytical direction you want to take, but you want just the right words to communicate your ideas. To stay with the map analogy one more time: in this case, you know the route from point A to point B, but you are just not sure about whether to take the highway or the scenic country road.

Where do I begin?

As you explore the inter-relationship between reading and writing within the discourse communities presented in this text, you will discover that you have many choices about how you can approach and navigate your way through the written conversation that is a part of that community. There are numerous ways that you can enter into a written conversation, and we call these entry points **portals**. Consider how Harry Potter, for example, in *The Goblet of Fire*, navigates his way into various locations; he finds those entrances or doorways that meet his demands.

If you think of the portal as a specific doorway, leading to all kinds of written destinations, then you may also consider how each portal carries its own unique set of templates that will get you to those destinations. Will some templates resemble others in various portals? Of course, but if the template itself acts as a type of road map, consider the portal to be the actual landscape itself—the territory upon which you now find yourself and are ready to explore.

Credits

Rhetorical Analysis

Finding the Portal

Top-Down Analysis

How you respond to matters of public concern often depends on the manner in which those matters are presented to you. Be it a general rallying his troops, an advocate pleading for her cause, a disenfranchised member seeking passage of a bill—all of these messages attempt to appeal to you through emotion or logic.

How you enter a conversation with the speaker of those concerns—either through an oral or written response—depends upon your ability to analyze the speaker's rhetoric, for through such analysis you demonstrate your understanding of what's being said and how it's being said. The **top-down analysis** most closely replicates the role of listener, one whose primary obligation is to follow the text (or speech) from beginning to end.

Political speeches—or texts with a timely, topical intent to persuade—present a greater emphasis on the bottom half of Aristotle's rhetorical triangle, as seen here:

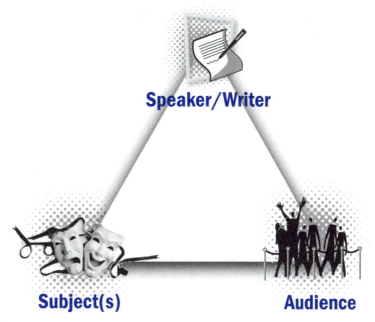

Speaker/Writer

Subject(s)   **Audience**

The Speaker/Writer strives to connect the Audience to the Subject(s).

Political speeches invite a "top-down" rhetorical analysis, whereby the reader starts at the top or beginning of the speech and works his or her way down, noting distinctive moves that the speaker (or writer) makes, and thereby emulates the experience of the audience.

The Reading Experience

The top-down analysis of rhetoric approaches the text from the beginning to the end. It is more than just a play-by-play analysis, however, as you must first have a sense of the overall purpose of the text. That purpose relates to the basic point or **message** that the author wants to convey. That purpose may be to warn of an impending danger, argue for the passage of certain laws or policies, or commemorate key events in the past or present, but behind good formal writing or speaking there is an exigent purpose in delivering that message. In some cases, the text will reveal such a message more explicitly, but often there is a more implicit message that reveals itself through analysis.

The Writing Experience

The top-down analysis also calls for a more expansive approach toward understanding an author's purpose. As you analyze text from top to bottom, you will discover as your analysis evolves how the writer's purpose evolves. Your own analysis becomes a new lens through which to view the original text. At the heart of rhetorical analysis lie two questions: **What is the author's message?** and **How is this message being communicated?** In the same manner in which you read a text from top to bottom, so, too, can your analysis follow a similar direction.

PORTAL POINTS FOR WRITING TOP-DOWN ANALYSIS:

The top-down analysis allows you to write a play-by-play analysis of the text and put yourself squarely in the role of the audience. Key points to consider as you write a top-down analysis are:

- the overall message or purpose of the text;
- the ways in which the message evolves;
- the techniques the writer/speaker employs in the service of this evolution.

To help you write a top-down analysis, examine the following templates. Think of these templates not only as a road map of what direction to take in your writing, but also as useful vocabulary for this direction.

Templates for Top-Down Rhetorical Analysis

▼ **Introducing the cause or exigence**
These templates introduce the writer's passion or reason for being.

The text's overall message or purpose is _____.

The speaker understands that _____ is at stake.

Within the context of _____, the writer argues for _____.

▼ **Acknowledging opposing views or concessions**
These templates introduce sensitivity for other sides and increase your own credibility.

By first acknowledging _____, the writer achieves _____.

Prior to arguing for _____, the speaker must first acknowledge _____.

The reason that the speaker begins with _____ is that _____.

It does seem paradoxical that the text would state _____, especially given _____.

The reasons that the writer argues for _____ become clear only when we reach the end of the text.

▼ **Refutations that build upon concession**
These templates allow you to thoughtfully balance all views with your own.

Once the opposite side has been recognized, the text can now more credibly address _____.

While the concession features a more conciliatory tone, the text shifts toward _____ in arguing for its point.

Now that the audience has been embraced through the concession, the writer can now make his main point that _____.

The writer achieves greater credibility by first conceding _____, which is then immediately followed with her main idea that _____.

While the concession relies more upon _____ [pick one: logic or emotion], the refutation works because it focuses the argument on [pick the other: logic or emotion].

▼ Analyzing how rhetorical moves inform meaning

These templates allow you to look at how a writer's technique aids in delivering a message.

The text furthers its argument of _____ with its use of *rhetorical move X.*

The introduction of *rhetorical move X* signals _____.

The movement from *rhetorical move X* to *rhetorical move Y* reflects the speaker's greater concern that _____.

By the next paragraph, the writer furthers his belief that _____. His primary method of doing this is through *rhetorical move X.*

▼ Analyzing how rhetoric builds

These templates allow you to look at the ways in which the text evolves from start to finish.

With this _____ tone, the speaker furthers his view that _____.

The text relies upon more than _____ appeal; it also includes _____ appeal.

The subject of the speech, however, is more than just _____; it is also _____.

The reason why _____ occurs later in the text is that _____.

The purpose finally becomes clearer when the writer states _____.

▼ Analyzing audience or public impact

These templates appear when the essay becomes a more expansive lens, where you write about the effect of the text.

On a larger scale, the writer is arguing for _____.

Though the speaker uses the first person, the argument applies to all because _____.

The broader appeal is found in _____.

By doing _____, the text succeeds in moving the discussion into a more universal realm.

By the conclusion, we know that the speaker has commented on more than just _____, but also _____.

Review these templates frequently, so that you can utilize their forms and content for future top-down analyses.

The Conversation Begins

A standard prompt for an essay of rhetorical analysis often features these two tasks:

• **Determine** the author's position on a given topic

• **Analyze** the rhetorical techniques he or she uses to achieve that position.

Notice how both of these tasks appear in the following prompt.

> Determine Barack Obama's main message(s) in his November 4, 2008, General Election Victory Speech, and analyze the techniques he uses to communicate that message.

To help you compose a successful essay in response to the prompt, complete the following steps.

Guided Practice

Step 1: *Reading the text*

Prior to writing about a text is the careful reading of that text. As you read the sample text, read also the accompanying annotations for an analysis of the rhetoric.

Excerpt from *Barack Obama's General Election Victory Speech November 4, 2008*

I was never the likeliest candidate for this office. We didn't start with much money or many endorsements. Our campaign was not hatched in the halls of Washington—it began in the backyards of Des Moines and the living rooms of Concord and the front porches of
5 Charleston.

It was built by working men and women who dug into what little savings they had to give five dollars and ten dollars and twenty dollars to this cause. It grew strength from the young people who rejected the myth of their generation's apathy; who left their homes and their
10 families for jobs that offered little pay and less sleep; from the not-so-young people who braved the bitter cold and scorching heat to knock on the doors of perfect strangers; from the millions of Americans who volunteered, and organized, and proved that more than two centuries later, a government of the people, by the people and for the people has
15 not perished from this Earth. This is your victory.

I know you didn't do this just to win an election and I know you didn't do it for me. You did it because you understand the enormity of the task that lies ahead. For even as we celebrate tonight, we know the challenges that tomorrow will bring are the greatest of our lifetime—

Rhetorical annotation

Concessions through the words **never** and **didn't** acknowledge the opposition to his candidacy and his underdog status.

Parallelism invokes different kinds of people and occupations.

The distinctive use of pronouns establishes the speaker's relationship directly with his audience. Note the movement toward we, or unity.

20 two wars, a planet in peril, the worst financial crisis in a century. Even as we stand here tonight, we know there are brave Americans waking up in the deserts of Iraq and the mountains of Afghanistan to risk their lives for us. There are mothers and fathers who will lie awake after their children fall asleep and wonder how they'll make the mort-

25 gage, or pay their doctors' bills, or save enough for college. There is new energy to harness and new jobs to be created; new schools to build and threats to meet and alliances to repair.

The road ahead will be long. Our climb will be steep. We may not get there in one year or even one term, but America—I have never

30 been more hopeful than I am tonight that we will get there. I promise you—we as a people will get there.

There will be setbacks and false starts. There are many who won't agree with every decision or policy I make as President, and we know that government can't solve every problem. But I will always be honest

35 with you about the challenges we face. I will listen to you, especially when we disagree. And above all, I will ask you join in the work of remaking this nation the only way it's been done in America for two hundred and twenty-one years—block by block, brick by brick, calloused hand by calloused hand.

40 What began twenty-one months ago in the depths of winter must not end on this autumn night. This victory alone is not the change we seek—it is only the chance for us to make that change. And that cannot happen if we go back to the way things were. It cannot happen without you.

45 So let us summon a new spirit of patriotism; of service and responsibility where each of us resolves to pitch in and work harder and look after not only ourselves, but each other. Let us remember that if this financial crisis taught us anything, it's that we cannot have a thriving Wall Street while Main Street suffers—in this country, we rise or fall

50 as one nation; as one people.

Let us resist the temptation to fall back on the same partisanship and pettiness and immaturity that has poisoned our politics for so long. Let us remember that it was a man from this state who first carried the banner of the Republican Party to the White House—a party

55 founded on the values of self-reliance, individual liberty, and national unity. Those are values we all share, and while the Democratic Party has won a great victory tonight, we do so with a measure of humility and determination to heal the divides that have held back our progress. As Lincoln said to a nation far more divided than ours, "We are

60 not enemies, but friends . . . though passion may have strained it must not break our bonds of affection." And to those Americans whose support I have yet to earn—I may not have won your vote, but I hear your voices, I need your help, and I will be your President too.

The metaphor of a journey invokes an experience that extends beyond the immediate.

The shift in tone is presented purposefully, in order to build to a more inspirational ending.

Invocation of the past provides historical context.

Step 2: *Pre-writing*

Discourse Questions To help you begin writing about the text, answer the following questions:

1. What is the exigence or urgent concern of this text?

2. What is the writer's message or purpose, and how does this message evolve?

3. In what way(s) does the speaker embrace his opponents?

4. Where do we see appeals to pathos? ethos? logic?

5. What features of the text's organization enhance its effectiveness?

6. What elements of language—especially diction, syntax, and metaphor—enhance the overall message?

7. Where does the tone shift? From what to what?

8. Who is the audience, and how does awareness of this audience impact the overall speech?

Notice how the discourse questions develop from the two basic questions: What is the author's message? (Questions 1-2) and How is this message being communicated? (Questions 3 through 8). This latter set of questions asks you to consider rhetorical devices or moves that the author made to engage the listener more actively. At this point in your analysis, you are answering two related but different questions: (a) What rhetorical move is the writing making? And (b) What is the effect of that move?

Record your observations in a 3-column chart, represented below:

What the author is saying?	How the author is saying it?	What are the effects of the author's moves?

Step 3: *Writing and integrating templates*

Listening In Let's listen to how one voice may use the templates in a sample analysis of the speech and its rhetorical techniques.

Sample response to Obama's Victory Speech prompt

How best to make a victory a celebration for an entire country, as opposed to for just one party? Barack Obama's celebration speech at Grant Park in Chicago, Illinois, demonstrates that celebration ultimately comes second to service, and that even at his most shining moment, his overall purpose is to create a vision that will move his country in a unified direction.

By first acknowledging his outsider status, Obama achieves greater credibility; he claims he was not the "likeliest of candidates" and that his campaign began in cities far outside of the nation's capital. This concession does more than to state his underdog role; the concession allows for his opposition to consider the myriad reasons his candidacy was "unlikely," and by not specifying what this feature was—race, status, experience, ideology—he resists limiting the victory to a single dimension. It is not just a Democratic victory, a black victory, an outsider's victory, and so on.

Identification of templates

*This template introduces his purpose. The actual word **purpose** signals your answer to the discourse question.*

*This template introduces the concession **and** its effect.*

*This template explains the **reasons** for the concession.*

Commentary

Observe how the templates provide the writer with a way to notice the rhetorical moves that Obama makes in his speech, and how the analysis notes the effect and/or significance of those moves. In each of the samples above, the success of the sentence depends upon the writer's ability to read and interpret the text accurately. The "blank" portion of the template demands that you fill it with key details. For example, the first template used is:

The text's overall message or purpose is _____.

The actual response, however, *builds* on this template and reads:

. . . that even at his most shining moment, <u>his overall purpose is to create a vision that will move his country in a unified direction</u>.

Also, notice how the templates appear in three different locations in the above samples. They may conclude a paragraph, transition into a new paragraph, or introduce an idea within a paragraph. For example, the second template serves as a transitional device, in order to introduce the new paragraph. The actual template used is:

By first acknowledging _____, the writer achieves _____.

The actual response again *builds* upon the template:

> <u>By first acknowledging his outsider status, Obama achieves greater credibility</u>; he claims he was not the "likeliest of candidates"

And the final template used actually occurs *within* a paragraph.

Guided Practice

Step 4: *Application of templates*

You Try It Up until now, you have been a listener. Now it is your turn to enter the conversation. On a separate page, continue the analysis of the Obama speech by answering the prompt for this section. Return to your graphic organizer from Step 2 to assist you here. As you work your way down the text, determine the moves the writer is making and the effects of those moves on the writer's overall purpose. Then, look at the catalogue of templates for the top-down rhetorical analysis located on pages 3 and 4 to help you construct key sentences in your response.

Excerpt for Practice

It was built by working men and women who dug into what little savings they had to give five dollars and ten dollars and twenty dollars to this cause. It drew strength from the young people who rejected the myth of their generation's apathy; who left their homes and their
10   families for jobs that offered little pay and less sleep; from the not-so-young people who braved the bitter cold and scorching heat to knock on the doors of perfect strangers; from the millions of Americans who volunteered, and organized, and proved that more than two centuries later, a government of the people, by the people and for the people has
15   not perished from this Earth. This is your victory.

Write your response and compare it with the following:

> ***Continuation of sample response to Obama's Victory Speech prompt***
>
> The speech builds upon its belief in unity in the next paragraph, as Obama's parallelism lists supporters who encompass a range of Americans who braved dire conditions to support his candidacy. These conditions, listed as an accumulation of increasingly difficult circumstances, reinforce the image of an American who has less financial power. Obama's diction moves from objects of apathy and discomfort—money, bitter cold, strangers—and then returns to verbs of strength: volunteer, organize, prove. In so doing, Obama reveals the American spirit to revive itself under difficult times, and by ending the sentence with a reference to Lincoln's Gettysburg Address, the parallels of a nation divided and the potential for a government to solve this are drawn. On a larger scale, Obama is calling for unity, much as Lincoln did.

This template joins purpose and rhetorical technique.

This template joins technique and purpose.

Commentary

The first template addresses the two fundamental questions of analysis: what is being said—in this case, a call for "unity," and how it is being said—in this case, through the use of parallelism. The template also prepares the reader for another aspect of content: the Americans who "braved dire conditions" to celebrate.

The second template connects key images of the speech to present a contrast—the "bitter cold," for example, versus the willingness of his audience to "volunteer" or "prove."

The remainder of the sample top-down analysis appears below. As you read it, make note of any places in the essay where you think the writer has incorporated templates for any aspect of rhetorical analysis.

Remainder of sample response to Obama's Victory Speech prompt

Choosing to acknowledge these difficult times, Obama's shift to a more urgent tone reveals his willingness to confront these challenges head on. Once he has worked to gain all of his audience through his rhetoric, his speech can now turn to the more difficult work ahead. Again, the use of parallelism reveals how the difficulties today strike everyone: he begins by referring to soldiers who sacrifice in Iraq; he moves to parents worrying about paying their mortgage; he names the global energy crisis. By finishing with a statement about the Earth, Obama identifies the importance for everyone to have a stake in tomorrow's decisions. His use of pronouns also reveals his ability to move his audience into a more public awareness. He says, "I know you didn't do this for me . . . or to win an election." The use of the first person presents a more humble, invitational aspect, and by naming what "you" voted for—that is, something more than just a person or an election—he extends the relationship of "I to you" as one that more aptly means "President to the electorate." Indeed, as the speech progresses, his reference to "you" shifts to "America."

Once the difficulties have been named, the speaker presents a vision that also relies upon metaphor, creativity, and imagination. "The road ahead will be long. Our climb will be steep." This abrupt syntax emphasizes the singularity of the mission. The purposeful ambiguity allows for further concession, as Obama notes that we may not get there in a single term, and it certainly will not be easy; by so doing, he continues to emphasize that the work is not about a single person or party, but that we are all obliged to participate. This is somewhat ironic to mention in a victory speech where optimism would rank high, yet Obama channels this optimism back to his audience. His reference to "calloused hand" invokes an image of hardworking Americans not afraid to confront difficulties, and there is an inspirational element in this difficult journey that lies ahead.

As Obama's vision for tomorrow builds toward a climactic moment, his use of parallelism joins the negative to the positive, and he presents a mechanism by which we Americans can start to consider our conditions today in a new light. Our situation embraces not just "ourselves" but "each other," not just "Wall Street" but "Main Street," not "partisanship and pettiness" but "friends." His return to Lincoln's address is a remarkable one, for it acknowledges that difficulties can exist, but it must not break the bonds of "affection." The use of this word invokes a degree of brotherhood and humanity, and the President-elect is conceding that while conflicts exist we must abide by our more humane side—an ironic choice, given his earlier references to wars in Iraq and Afghanistan, as well as "the worst" financial crisis in our nation's history. Indeed, by calling out to those Americans "whose support [he] has yet to earn," Obama continues to concede that he has his opponents, but that he is working toward their approval. While this excerpt began with a concession that invokes the negative, this concluding statement is more inclusive, rather than exclusive, and the everyman theme is again reinstilled.

Wrapping Up the Portal As you can see, the top-down analysis proceeds in a linear fashion through the document under discussion. But sometimes the most effective analysis results from looking at particular strategies wherever they appear in the work, and so you might want to enter the task through a different portal, the analysis by technique.

Analysis by Technique

When examining an individual's rhetoric, we do more than just explore the public concerns or arguments that frequently appear in the news. We may wish to enter a written conversation when we come across a writer who reflects in a personal way upon situations, experiences, or ideas that contain more universal concerns. We may find ourselves drawn to a writer's reflection on an outdoor experience that has broader implications, a diarist's observations about internment that reflects a deeper truth about the nature of humanity, or a satirist's speech that not only parodies a well known figure but also forces an audience to reconsider a previously held opinion. Often, these reflections appear in memoir, reflections, journals, and columns. Their use of argument is subtler, more implicit, and often more personal than that found in speeches or political pamphlets.

Unlike your response to more public or political texts, where you are particularly attentive to the ways in which the speaker carefully understands his relationship with the subject and audience, your response to more private texts, such as memoir, places greater emphasis on the ways in which you perceive the writer presenting himself or herself. Such a response invites an analysis by technique, whereby you still examine what is being said and how it is being said, but you focus less on audience and more on the techniques the writer uses to present his or her subjects.

The memoirist, unlike the political speaker, presents a text that is less committed to audience—not that he or she does not care about the audience—but the sheer act of creating memoir presupposes a greater permanence, something that aspires to a goal more commonly associated with fiction. To that end, the analysis of memoir, literary journalism, editorials, and newspaper columns places greater emphasis on the moves of the writer, as well as the subjects he or she is presenting. To return to Aristotle's rhetorical triangle, where Top-Down Analysis emphasizes subject(s) and audience, **analysis by technique** emphasizes subject(s) and writer.

The word "essay" comes from a French word that means "to try." Many of our best known essayists, beginning with the great French writer Michel de Montaigne (1533–1592), present their arguments in a format where the purpose is revealed only at the end of the essay, and often it is presented in a highly sophisticated manner. While *public* rhetoric manipulates the audience in bold strokes, this more *private* rhetoric manipulates the audience in nuanced strokes.

This more private rhetoric lends itself effectively to an analysis by technique. Like the top-down analysis, you still have an obligation to understand what the exigence is, but because of the more intimate nature of this text, what deserves greater attention in this analysis is the technique the writer employs to convey his or her message. This is not to suggest that somehow the message is less important than in public discourse, nor is it to suggest that the public speech somehow lacks rhetorical finesse; indeed, narrative can produce an argument as nuanced as a political speech. But with more nuanced arguments, you may have to work harder to explicate the writer's moves.

Regardless of the approach you take in analysis, your first task is to determine what the overall purpose of the text is. *The method of analysis you choose should illuminate your comprehension of what a text's message is and the rhetorical moves the author uses to convey that message.*

The Writing Experience

In the same manner in which you read a text with attention to its technique, so, too, can your written approach follow a similar direction.

PORTAL POINTS FOR ANALYSIS BY TECHNIQUE:

The analysis by technique approach allows you to focus on the ways in which a writer's artistry furthers his or her message. Key points to consider when you are writing the analysis by technique are:

- the implicit and/or explicit messages of the text;
- the remarkable features of the text present in the writing;
- the ways in which key features or ideas *accumulate* from start to finish.

To help you write analysis by technique, examine the following templates. Think of these templates not only as a road map of what direction to take in your writing, but also as a useful vocabulary for this direction.

Templates for Rhetorical Analysis by Technique

▼ Identifying the purpose

These templates introduce the purpose of the text, which may be more explicitly or implicitly stated, or both.

The author's journey reflects the larger truth that _____.

While the narrative focuses on a single instance of _____, the message of _____ extends to all.

At the beginning of the text, the author poses a conflict regarding _____; by the end, the author's answer is _____.

As the author herself indicates, her purpose in this text is _____. But there is a larger application to her text, one that asks readers to consider _____.

The writer's purpose in this text is to _____.

▼ Templates that blend technique and content

These templates look at the relationship between what a writer says and what technique he or she uses or how it is said.

The author's message of _____ is reinforced by her use of *rhetorical technique X*.

The author's reliance upon *rhetorical technique X* suggests her belief that _____.

Rhetorical technique X, commonly associated with *desired effect Y*, illuminates this message.

As a result of _____, the text incorporates *rhetorical technique X* as a means to achieve *desired effect Y*.

By introducing *rhetorical technique X*, the writer achieves *desired effect Y*. This influences the message to become _____.

The evolution of *rhetorical technique Y* from beginning to end reflects a similar evolution of the message.

▼ Incorporating a second rhetorical technique

These templates allow you to combine techniques in a single paragraph.

In addition to *rhetorical technique X*, the author's incorporation of *rhetorical technique Y* furthers the message that _____.

Rhetorical techniques X and Y interact to produce *desired effect Z*.

Of equal impact is the text's use of *rhetorical technique Y*, for the message of the text also addresses _____.

Most noteworthy about the language of the piece is that _____.

When the tone shifts from _____ to _____, the message becomes clear: _____.

The change in the language parallels the author's purpose in showing _____.

Later in the text, however, the *rhetorical technique X* gives way to *rhetorical technique Y*, as if to suggest that _____.

Contrasts in imagery are also accompanied by contrasts in _____. The reason for this is that _____.

The reason that the message shifts is that _____.

Only by viewing the moment from a contrasting perspective can the author realize _____.

By the end of the piece, the *rhetorical technique X* has shifted from _____ to _____, as if to suggest _____.

The writer reveals her clear purpose when she states _____.

By first establishing an appropriate context for his message, the author is finally able to articulate his main purpose: _____.

The author cannot come out and directly state _____ because _____.

The text gradually builds to the idea that _____.

Has the writer come full circle by the end? Or has she moved forward? The ending suggests _____.

The ending of the text presents a dilemma when compared to the beginning because _____.

The Conversation Begins

While on the surface analysis by technique appears identical to top-down analysis, the emphasis is slightly different. While you are still looking at the connection between form and content in this portal, with analysis by technique, form takes on greater prominence.

A standard prompt reads as follows:

In the following excerpt, the author reveals his or her views on a key concept. **Determine** what **the writer's views** are, as well as the **techniques** used to communicate these views.

For this exercise, the prompt is:

> Read the following excerpt from *The Color of Water* by James McBride. Analyze the author's views on empathy and the rhetorical techniques he uses to develop these views.

To help you compose a successful essay in response to the prompt, complete the following steps.

Guided Exercise

Step 1: *Reading the text*

Read the following excerpt from a memoir, and see how the templates would operate in response to writing about this memoir. As you read the sample text, read also the accompanying annotations for an analysis of the rhetoric.

The following excerpt is from James McBride's 1996 memoir *The Color of Water*. McBride recounts his childhood experience as an African-American son of a Jewish mother, who has just been sold rotten milk at a store.

The Color of Water

Rhetorical annotation

I thought the man would see Ma, think they had something in common, then give her the dough and we'd be off. "That milk is sold," he said.

"Smell it," Ma said. "It's spoiled."

5   "I don't smell milk. I sell milk."

Is there a symbolic value to spoiled milk that McBride provides?

Right away they were at each other, I mean really going at it. A crowd of black kids gathered, watching my white mother arguing with this white man. I wanted to sink into the floor and disappear. "It's okay, Ma . . . " I said. She ignored me. In matters of money, of which

10   she had so little, I knew it was useless. She was going full blast—"… fool…think you…idiot!"—her words flying together like gibberish, while the neighborhood kids howled, woofing like dogs and enjoying the show.

After a while it was clear the man was not going to return her
15 money, so she grabbed my hand and was heading toward the door,
when he made another remark, something that I missed, something
he murmured beneath his breath so softly that I couldn't hear, but
it made the crowd murmur "Ooohhh." Ma stiffened. Still holding the
milk in her right hand, she turned around and flung it at him like a
20 football. He ducked and the milk missed him, smashing into the cigarette cabinet behind him and sending milk and cigarettes splattering
everywhere.

I could not understand such anger. I could not understand why
she didn't just give up the milk. Why cause a fuss? I thought. My own
25 embarrassment overrode all other feelings. As I walked home, holding Mommy's hand while she fumed, I thought it would be easier if
we were just one color, black or white. I didn't want to be white. My
siblings had already instilled the notion of black pride in me. I would
have preferred that Mommy were black. Now, as a grown man, I feel
30 privileged to have come from two worlds. My view of the world is not
merely that of a black man but that of a black man with something
of a Jewish soul. I don't consider myself Jewish, but when I look at
Holocaust photographs of Jewish women whose children have been
wrenched from them by Nazi soldiers, the women look like my own
35 mother and I think to myself, *There but for the grace of God goes my
own mother—and by extension, myself.* When I see two little Jewish old ladies giggling over coffee at a Manhattan diner, it makes me
smile, because I hear my own mother's laughter beneath theirs. Conversely, when I hear black "leaders" talking about "Jewish slave own-
40 ers" I feel angry and disgusted, knowing that they're inflaming people
with lies and twisted history, as if all seven of the Jewish slave owners in the antebellum South, or however few there were, are responsible for the problems of African-Americans now. Those leaders are
no better than their Jewish counterparts who spin statistics in mar-
45 velous ways to make African-Americans look like savages, criminals,
drags on society, and "animals" (a word quite popular when used to
describe blacks these days). I don't belong to any of those groups. I
belong to the world of one God, one people. But as a kid, I preferred
the black side, and often wished that Mommy had sent me to black
50 schools like my friends. Instead I was stuck at that white school, P.S.
138, with white classmates who were convinced I could dance like
James Brown. They constantly badgered me to do the "James Brown"
for them, a squiggling of the feet made famous by the "Godfather of
Soul" himself, who back in the sixties was bigger than life. I tried to
55 explain to them that I couldn't dance. I have always been one of the
worst dancers that God has ever put upon this earth. My sisters would
spend hours at home trying out new dances to Archie Bell and the

The narrative builds tension here, and the simile of a "football" mixes the game with aggression.

The speaker positions himself within a larger context of religion, history, and race.

The use of contrasts in language reflect multiple cultures and attitudes.

60 Drells, Martha Reeves, King Curtis, Curtis Mayfield, Aretha Franklin, and the Spinners. "Come on and dance!" they'd shout, boogying across the room. Even Ma would join in, sashaying across the floor, but when I joined in I looked so odd and stupid they fell to the floor laughing, "Give it up," they said. "You can't dance."

65 The white kids in school did not believe me, and after weeks of encouragement I found myself standing in front of the classroom on talent day, wearing my brother's good shoes and hitching up my pants, soul singer-style like one of the Temptations, as someone dropped the needle on a James Brown record. I slid around the way I'd seen him do, shouting "Owww—shabba-na!" They were delighted. Even the teacher was amused. They really believed I could dance! I had them
70 fooled. They screamed for more and I obliged, squiggling my feet and slip-sliding across the wooden floor, jumping into the air and landing in a near split by the blackboard, shouting "Eeee-yowwww!" They went wild, but even as I sat down with their applause ringing in my ears, with laughter on my face, happy to feel accepted, to be part of them,
75 knowing I had pleased them, I saw the derision on their faces, the clever smiles, laughing at the oddity of it, and I felt the same ache I felt when I gazed at the boy in the mirror. I remember him, and how free he was, I hated him even more. (1996)

James McBride

The ending here is ambivalent. Has the writer given an explicit statement of purpose, or does he wish his readers to see something he himself cannot?

Step 2: *Pre-writing*

Discourse Questions To help you begin writing about the text, answer the following questions:

1. What words or phrases best illustrate the speaker or other people?

2. What is remarkable about the diction, syntax, and/or imagery?

3. On a literal level, what is the conflict about? On a symbolic level, what is the conflict about?

4. What is the author's argument here?

5. Find one line that best illuminates the author's purpose or exigence. Is the author's thesis implicit or explicit?

6. To what extent does the ending of the passage reveal a change from the persona presented in the first part of the passage?

7. How is the narrative representative a larger concern?

8. Where do any shifts in tone, mood, or pacing occur?

At this point in your analysis, you are answering two related but different questions: a) what rhetorical move is the writer making; and, b) what is the effect of that move?

Record your observations in a 3-column chart similar to the one found on page 7, and compare your responses to the one that follows.

Guided Practice

Step 3: *Writing and integrating templates*

Listening In Let's listen to the voice of one writer who used the sample templates to analyze the ways in which McBride communicates his views on empathy.

Sample response to James McBride prompt

James McBride's journey in his memoir *The Color of Water* reveals that empathy for others' differences requires more than living under the same roof; empathy for others begins first with an understanding and acceptance of one's self. His account of his conflict with his mother and the store clerk, while illustrative of destructive racism, parallels his own willingness to debase his own identity to please others in school, as if to suggest that the conformity that defines us as youngsters only comes back to haunt us as adults.

The metaphoric language throughout McBride's memoir conveys the ambiguity and uncertainty of identifying one's self by race or religion. The passage's opening reference to "spoiled milk" represents two things: one, the store owner's unwillingness to treat a white mother fairly, for the simple reason that she has a black child; two, the store owner's view of this woman as somehow spoiled, for she has been saddled with a black child, in the store owner's eyes. These symbols become strangely real when McBride recounts the stereotypical views of various ethnicities: Jews as "slave holders" and blacks as "animals," as if to suggest that the labels we give food are no different from the labels we give human beings. Noteworthy is McBride's diction, where he describes the children as "woofing like dogs" at the opening conflict between his mother and the store owner. Such confusion over one's identity is finally manifested by the end of the passage, as the author characterizes himself as someone else—James Brown—gyrating, moving, behaving like someone he is not. The text finally refers to "The Temptations," a popular music group for their era, but more aptly a title suited to the writer's inability to withstand the lure of classmates who will accept him only if he validates their perceptions of what a cool black person is.

Identification of templates

This template describes the overall journey that a memoirist is describing, along with the impact of that journey.

This template focuses on the ways in which technique (how something is said) informs purpose (what's being said).

This template introduces a rhetorical technique within the paragraph.

In analysis by technique, you can look for places where the end of the text speaks to the beginning of the text.

Commentary

The work of the template is only the training wheel. In each of the templates identified on pages 17 and 18, the success of the sentence depends upon your ability to read and interpret the text accurately. The "blank" portion of the template demands your creative interaction with text.

Also, you should note that the templates appear in three different locations in the above samples. Here, they introduce the entire essay, occur within a paragraph, and conclude a paragraph.

Remember that the templates can be as much thinking guides as actual vocabulary terms. Note this template that connects technique and content:

By introducing *rhetorical technique X*, the writer achieves ***desired effect Y***. This influences the message to become _____.

The line of the actual response reads:

> The metaphoric language throughout McBride's memoir conveys the ambiguity and uncertainty of identifying one's self by race or religion.

And now consider another way the same template is used in the sample above:

> Noteworthy is McBride's diction, where he describes the children as "woofing like dogs" at the opening conflict between his mother and the store owner.

Guided Practice

Step 4: *Application of templates*

You Try It Now it is your turn to enter the conversation. In your notebook, continue the analysis of the McBride piece by focusing on the technique or language that creates the mood.

Return to your 3-column chart from Step 2 to assist you here. As you work your way down the text, determine the moves the writer is making and the effects of those moves on the writer's overall purpose. Then, look at the catalogue of templates for rhetorical analysis by technique located on pages 14 and 15 to help you construct key sentences in your response.

Excerpt for Practice

The white kids in school did not believe me, and after weeks of encouragement I found myself standing in front of the classroom on
65 talent day, wearing my brother's good shoes and hitching up my pants, soul singer-style like one of the Temptations, as someone dropped the needle on a James Brown record. I slid around the way I'd seen him do, shouting "Owww—shabba-na!" They were delighted. Even the teacher was amused. They really believed I could dance! I had them
70 fooled. They screamed for more and I obliged, squiggling my feet and slip-sliding across the wooden floor, jumping into the air and landing in a near split by the blackboard, shouting "Eeee-yowwww!" They went wild, but even as I sat down with their applause ringing in my ears, with laughter on my face, happy to feel accepted, to be part of them,
75

75 knowing I had pleased them, I saw the derision on their faces, the clever smiles, laughing at the oddity of it, and I felt the same ache I felt when I gazed at the boy in the mirror. I remember him, and how free he was, I hated him even more.

Write your response in your notebook. Underline the templates you used and explain why you used them. Then compare your response with the one below.

Continuation of sample response to James McBride prompt

Such ambiguity over self-acceptance is furthered by the uneven mood of the piece. The change in the mood reflects the author's ambivalence about his identity. What should end with reconciliation and assuredness is rather a false complacency, suggesting that the author may be able to intellectually understand his discomfort over racism, but he is powerless to act differently in its presence. At the beginning of the passage, the abrupt syntax punctuates the uncomfortable mood: "She ignored me." "Ma stiffened." "Why cause a fuss?" His mother's refusal to be intimidated by a racist store owner causes her to lash out, unlike the author who quietly acquiesces. The howling at the beginning of the text is echoed by additional howling at the end, except by the end, the author has chosen to entertain others, as opposed to confronting the dark truths that his mother does at the beginning of the passage. Again, the abrupt syntax serves to highlight finality: "They were delighted." "I had them fooled." The reason the mood shifts is to convey something opposite to reassurance: resignation and defeat.

Identification of templates

This template introduces a contrast.

This template connects technique with effect.

This is another template to explain contrast.

Commentary

In addition to using templates as transitions among paragraphs, templates can also be used within a paragraph itself, especially as you achieve greater coherence. Note that in the above example, the first and last templates comment on a shift—in mood and self-image. In analyzing McBride's growing awareness of racial identity, this essay features the transition of McBride's self-image through templates that encourage communicating the nature of that shift.

The remainder of the sample analysis by technique appears below. Make note of those parts of the essay which you think incorporate templates for any aspect of rhetorical analysis.

Remainder of sample response to James McBride prompt

If a solution to the dangers of conformity does exist, argues McBride, then it comes with age and understanding. The author's balance of formal and informal language reflects this perspective. His adult reflection on the extremities of stereotyping establishes a context for his childhood conflicts. His references to Nazism and slavery show that he understands the irrationality of prejudice, and McBride parallels these historical tragedies with his modern-day conflict. And while he also notes the similarities in prejudicial behavior towards blacks and Jews, he also understands how these two conflicts are irreconcilable toward each other. He notes that prejudicial black "leaders are no better than their Jewish counterparts who spin statistics in marvelous ways to make African-Americans look like savages, criminals, drags on society, and 'animals' (a word quite popular when used to describe blacks these days). I don't belong to any of those groups." The parallelism—again culminating in "animals"—reflects his disdain for the racism. But the abrupt disavowal suggests that the author places himself somewhere between these two extremities, a wish to be free of the historical pull that tears him and his family apart.

Amid this intellectual awareness, however, comes the realization that such a journey takes a lifetime, and much of the speaker's youth is characterized by acquiescence toward popular culture. While referring to others who "inflame" or "spin statistics," McBride himself "boogies," "shouts," and "slides," actions somewhat reminiscent of the young children characterized at the beginning of the passage. And even his use of the word "derision" by the end of the text reflects his inability to act beyond understanding, as though he is stuck in his damaging conformity.

In a text that reveals conflict over identity, the author's own use of contrasts perhaps best illustrates the difficulties of self-acceptance, but this contrast also enriches who the speaker is. In addition to the conflict between black and white, McBride writes about Jews versus Nazis, age versus youth, acceptance versus derision, and private versus public dignity. His final image of hating the reflection in the mirror illuminates how these contrasts struggle to define the speaker, but they also offer a ray of hope, as if to suggest that the dissatisfaction that McBride feels when he looks at himself in the mirror spurs him toward continuing the journey of self-discovery.

Wrapping Up the Portal While a text may be accessed through various portals, the context of the writing often guides you to the portal, and with a more personal context—such as a memoir—an analysis by technique may produce a significantly different essay than a top-down analysis. Other analytical approaches are also possible, and you are about to see a third kind of analytical essay, the kind that evaluates an argument.

Portal 3

Finding the Portal

The Reading Experience

The Writing Experience

Evaluation of an Argument

In addition to analyzing the rhetorical strategies of an argument, you may also encounter the task of an **evaluation of an argument**. When you evaluate, you judge, and this means that your opinion must be an informed one. While evaluations do communicate whether you agree or disagree, or whether or not an argument is sound, to enter a written conversation that involves judging is a more difficult task, for an informed opinion depends upon an accurate analysis.

Perhaps one way to view this portal is to consider that a written *analysis* is a one-way street where you enter the conversation by presenting your observations. But when you provide a written *evaluation*, you prepare the way for a two-way street, whereby your participation responds directly to another party, and in doing so, you have moved beyond *entering* the conversation into *engaging* the conversation. To return to Aristotle's rhetorical triangle, the emphasis here is on the audience relating to the speaker/writer.

Essays that evaluate arguments act as a type of hybrid between the more public discourse examples—such as a rallying cry, an election speech, a eulogy—and the more private experiences—such as memoir, reflection, or journal. You are given the time, the space, and most important, the charge to determine whether or not an argument is a valid one. When Abraham Lincoln delivered his Gettysburg Address, listeners had a sense that it was an epochal moment, but it was not until generations later that a fuller appreciation of the rhetoric came to the fore.

Conversely, it was the Allied Powers' failure to correctly evaluate appeasement claims for Alsace-Lorraine that contributed to the conflagration of World War II.

These two examples above, however, suggest that the evaluation of an argument does lead to a correct answer, which is not always the case. Witness today's controversial issues with no clear "right answer": wars in Iraq or Afghanistan, a financial meltdown, automobile companies threatening to go out of business, global warming. In all controversial issues proponents develop arguments for or against a position on a topic, or why we should or should not pursue a particular course of action.

Unlike the examples from political or private discourse, the evaluation of an argument already accepts a level of controversy over a given topic. The prior examples rely less upon ambiguity. You know what a candidate wants; you can interpret the memoir's larger purpose. There is less at stake in terms of the audience's ability to understand.

For example, in analyzing a political speech, you can accurately address the ways in which an audience would be swayed. The greatest variable to address in the rhetorical triangle is the *speaker or writer*. And with a memoir, while there may be more uncertainty when it comes to targeting an author's larger purpose, the greatest variable comes not with audience, but with the *subject*.

But with the evaluation of an argument, the greatest variable is with the *audience*. If you are to have a voice and a stake in the conversation—important responsibilities for informed readers and writers—then it is incumbent upon you to develop an informed opinion.

So, the occasions for evaluating an argument would likely be current, controversial statements on subjects that clearly have more than one perspective.

The evaluation of an argument exists somewhere between the receiver and the sender of the argument, a type of buffer zone in which the argument can be distilled and processed before returning to the public domain.

The process for evaluation, too, exists somewhere between a top-down analysis and an analysis by technique. You would avoid working your way down the speech piece by piece, as you are addressing various stages of the argument throughout. At the same time, all arguments rest upon an equation of claims, qualifiers, evidence, and conclusions, so you are obliged to follow the course of the argument—at least in parts. Perhaps it is easiest to think of this approach like highway construction. Sections of the road are worked on at a time, but rarely are these sections worked on in sequential order.

PORTAL POINTS FOR EVALUATION OF ARGUMENT:

In the same manner in which you evaluate an argument, so, too, can your written response follow a similar direction. The evaluation approach allows you to judge the merits of a given argument. Key points to consider when writing an evaluation of argument are:

- the position or the message;
- the ways in which the message is communicated;
- your own judgment on the credibility, logic, or value of either argument.

To help you write an evaluation of argument, examine the following templates. Think of these templates not only as a road map of what direction to take in your writing, but also as useful vocabulary for this direction.

Templates for Evaluation of an Argument

> These words convey your judgment on the causes, effects, or activities that describe how others have already entered into this particular conversation.

Adverbs to convey evaluation

Correctly	Effectively	Adequately	Successfully	Squarely
Aptly	Insufficiently	Naively	Poorly	Foolishly

Adjectives to convey evaluation

Accurate	Credible	Illogical	Fallacious	Faulty
Cogent	Untenable	Good	Limited	Persuasive

Verbs to convey evaluation

Fails	Succeeds	Assumes	Disregards	Ignores
Honors	Achieves	Maintains	Validates	Risks

Introducing an evaluation
These templates reveal your own evaluation and position.

The author correctly argues that _____.

Though the author fails to acknowledge _____, he does succeed in his argument for _____.

It is not the argument itself that lacks credibility, but the method by which this argument is presented that is faulty.

Though the speaker uses sound technique in the construction of his argument, his overall position is untenable, due to its controversial nature.

Templates that agree with the author's position
These templates show your agreement with the author or subject.

The speaker's belief that _____ rests upon his successful employment of logic and pathos.

It is difficult to argue with _____, given the effectiveness of the evidence.

The author presents a logical, cogent discussion on _____.

Though the writing relies too heavily upon *rhetorical technique X*, the overall position is tenable, given the effective use of *rhetorical technique Y*.

▼ Templates that disagree with parts of the author's position

These templates show your disagreement with the author or subject.

The speaker's belief that _____ is faulty, largely because of his failure to acknowledge _____.

Though the argument is airtight with respect to _____, other parts have flaws.

Given the highly sensitive nature of this topic, why does the author rely solely upon *rhetorical technique X* to make her point?

I would be tempted to agree with the argument, but there is a lack of compelling evidence.

Yes, the argument is airtight, but the writer has failed to represent how the opposition feels and therefore loses credibility.

▼ Identifying assumptions or faulty logic

These templates encourage you to look for logical fallacies, or areas where the argument is less credible.

The speaker makes a cause-effect relationship between _____ and _____, but this needs more proof.

The writer has whittled down this controversy into only two options: an either/or box. Is there not a third way of looking at it?

Just because this example worked for this speaker, does it truly speak for a larger constituency?

Has the argument really proven that if we do _____, then _____ will follow?

Yes, there are compelling examples from all over. But can we therefore deduce that _____ will follow?

The writer seems to have ignored the possibility of other examples; what about _____?

The speaker's assertion is correct even today. Look at _____.

The argument applies only to one sector of our society. Consider _____ as just one exception.

My own story corroborates much of what the text is arguing for.

One has only to look at _____ to see how valid this argument truly is.

Review these templates frequently, so that you can utilize their forms and content for future Evaluations of Arguments.

The Conversation Begins

A standard prompt that involves Evaluation of Argument often features these two tasks:

Determine the author's position on a given topic and **evaluate** the methods by which the argument is presented.

OR

Determine the author's position on a given topic and **evaluate** the validity of that claim.

OR

Evaluate the pros and cons of the author's argument, and **determine** which side is more persuasive.

Notice how both of these tasks appear in the following prompt.

The following text is an excerpt from an essay called "Dumpster Diving" by Lars Eighner. Read the text carefully. Then, in a well-organized essay, determine Eighner's position on self-reliance, and evaluate the cogency of his argument.

To help you compose a successful essay in response to this prompt, complete the following steps.

Step 1: *Reading the text*

Prior to writing about a text is the careful reading of the text. As you read the sample text, also read the accompanying annotations for an evaluation of argument.

Excerpt from "Dumpster Diving"

Rhetorical annotation

Dumpster things are often sad—abandoned teddy bears, shredded wedding books, despaired-of sales kits. I find many pets lying in state in Dumpsters. Although I hope to get off the streets so that Lizbeth can have a long and comfortable old age, I know this hope is not

5 very realistic. So I suppose when her time comes she too will go into a Dumpster. I will have no better place for her. And after all, it is fitting, since for most of her life her livelihood has come from the Dumpster. When she finds something I think is safe that has been spilled from a Dumpster, I let her have it. She already knows the route around

10 the best ones. I like to think that if she survives me she will have a chance of evading the dog catcher and of finding her sustenance on the route.

Silly vanities also come to rest in the Dumpsters. I am a rather accomplished needleworker. I get a lot of material from the Dump-

15 sters. Evidently sorority girls, hoping to impress someone, perhaps themselves, with their mastery of a womanly art, buy a lot of embroider-by-number kits, work a few stitches horribly, and eventually discard the whole mess. I pull out their stitches, turn the canvas over, and work an original design. Do not think I refrain from chuckling as

20 I make gifts from these kits.

I find diaries and journals. I have often thought of compiling a book of literary found objects. And perhaps I will one day. But what I find is hopelessly commonplace and bad without being, even unconsciously, camp. College students also discard their papers. I am hor-

25 rified to discover the kind of paper that now merits an A in an undergraduate course. I am grateful, however, for the number of good books and magazines the students throw out.

In the area I know best I have never discovered vermin in the Dumpsters, but there are two kinds of kitty surprise. One is alley cats

30 who I meet as they leap, claws first, out of Dumpsters. This is especially thrilling when I have Lizbeth in tow. The other kind of kitty surprise is a plastic garbage bag filled with some ponderous, amorphous mass. This always proves to be used cat litter.

City bees harvest doughnut glaze and this makes the Dumpster

35 at the doughnut shop more interesting. My faith in the instinctive wisdom of animals is always shaken whenever I see Lizbeth attempt

The passage begins provocatively, praising Dumpsters.

The inference here is that college students are frivolous and privileged; he has an almost condescending air.

Why the stark imagery? Is its intent to shock the reader? Or is he challenging us?

to catch a bee in her mouth, which she does wherever bees are present. Evidently some birds find Dumpsters profitable, for birdie surprise is almost as common as kitty surprise of the first kind. In hunt-
40 ing season all kinds of small game turn up in Dumpsters, some of it, sadly, not entirely dead. Curiously, summer and winter, maggots are uncommon.

There is a more playful nature here, one that belies the content.

The worst of the living and near-living hazards of the Dumpsters are the fire ants. The food they claim is not much of a loss, but they are
45 vicious and aggressive. It is very easy to brush against some surface of the Dumpster and pick up half a dozen or more fire ants, usually in some sensitive area such as the underarm. One advantage of bringing Lizbeth along as I make Dumpster rounds is that, for obvious reasons, she is very alert to ground-based fire ants. When Lizbeth recognizes
50 a fire-ant infestation around our feet, she does the Dance of the Zillion Fire Ants. I have learned not to ignore this warning from Lizbeth, whether I perceive the tiny ants or, not, but to remove ourselves at Lizbeth's first pas de bouree. All the more so because the ants are the worst in the summer months when I wear flip-flops if I have them.
55 (Perhaps someone will misunderstand this. Lizbeth does the Dance of the Zillion Fire Ants when she recognizes more fire ants than she cares to eat, not when she is being bitten. Since I have learned to react promptly, she does not get bitten at all. It is the isolated patrol of fire ants that falls in Lizbeth's range that deserves pity. She finds
60 them quite tasty.)

By far the best way to go through a Dumpster is to lower yourself into it. Most of the good stuff tends to settle at the bottom because it is usually weightier than the rubbish. My more athletic companions have often demonstrated to me that they can extract much good mate-
65 rial from a Dumpster I have already been over.

Does he really expect us to follow this? Or is he being ironic?

To those psychologically or physically unprepared to enter a Dumpster, I recommend a stout stick, preferable with some barb or hook at one end. The hook can be used to grab plastic garbage bags. When I find canned goods or other objects loose at the bottom of a
70 Dumpster, I lower a bag into it, roll the desired object into the bag, and then hoist the bag out—a procedure more easily described than executed. Much Dumpster diving is a matter of experience for which nothing will do except practice.

Dumpster diving is outdoor work, often surprisingly pleasant. It is
75 not entirely predictable; things of interest turn up every day and some days there are finds of great value. I am always very pleased when I can turn up exactly the thing I most wanted to find. Yet in spite of the element of chance, scavenging more than most other pursuits tends to yield returns in some proportion to the effort and intelligence brought
80 to bear. It is very sweet to turn up a few dollars in change from a Dumpster that has just been gone over by a wino.

His language is formal, articulate, balanced.

The land is now covered with cities. The cities are full of Dumpsters. If a member of the canine race is ever able to know what it is doing, then Lizbeth knows that when we go around to the Dumpsters,
85 we are hunting. I think of scavenging as a modern form of self-reliance. In any event, after having survived nearly ten years of government service, where everything is geared to the lowest common denominator, [it was not] work that rewards initiative and effort. Certainly I would be happy to have a sinecure again, but I am no longer heartbroken
90 that I left one.

I find from the experience of scavenging two rather deep lessons. The first is to take what you can use and let the rest go by. I have come to think that there is no value in the abstract. A thing I cannot use or make useful, perhaps by trading, has no value however rare or fine it
95 may be. I mean useful in a broad sense—some art I would find useful and some otherwise.

I was shocked to realize that some things are not worth acquiring, but now I think it is so. Some material things are white elephants that eat up the possessor's substance. The second lesson is the transience
100 of material being. This has not quite converted me to a dualist, but it has made some headway in that direction. I do not suppose that ideas are immortal, but certainly mental things are longer lived than other material things.

Once I was the sort of person who invests objects with sentimen-
105 tal value. Now I no longer have those objects, but I have the sentiments yet.

Many times in our travels I have lost everything but the clothes I was wearing and Lizbeth. The things I find in Dumpsters, the love letters and rag dolls of so many lives, remind me of this lesson. Now I
110 hardly pick up a thing without envisioning the time I will cast it aside. This I think is a healthy state of mind. Almost everything I have now has already been cast out at least once, proving that what I own is valueless to someone.

Anyway, I find my desire to grab for the gaudy bauble has been
115 largely sated. I think this is an attitude I share with the very wealthy— we both know there is plenty more where what we have came from. Between us are the rat-race millions who nightly scavenge the cable channels looking for they know not what.

I am sorry for them.

Lars Eighner

The allusion to Emerson's essay, and Thoreau's embodiment of it, as well as a jab on urban life, establishes a broader context for the argument.

Is this the explicit thesis?

Or this? It does seem plausible, that items are transient.

The final irony in comparison to the rich—"gaudy" is an appropriate symbol.

Is he patronizing at the end?

Step 2: *Pre-writing*

Discourse Questions To help you begin writing about the text, answer the following questions:

1. What is the author's argument? Is it explicit or implicit?

2. How credible is the speaker? What gives him or her credibility?

3. Examine the logic that the writer employs. Are there any gaps in the logic?

4. Does the argument rely upon any emotional appeals? If so, do they further the argument, or do they detract from the argument?

5. What assumptions does the writer make in terms of audience? In terms of content? Are these assumptions false?

6. Where do you find yourself agreeing with the writer? Why?

7. Where do you find yourself disagreeing with the writer? Why?

To help you organize your thoughts, record your answers to the pre-writing questions in a 3-column table, indicating the main points of the argument, the methods of development, and the areas of agreement and disagreement.

Remember, evaluation is adding your own judgment after you have analyzed; effective evaluation is a product of effective analysis.

Step 3: *Writing and integrating templates*

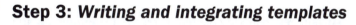

Listening In Let's listen to how one voice may use the templates in a sample analysis of the essay and its rhetorical techniques. Read the following sample response to the Lars Eighner piece, along with the ways in which templates assist the writing.

Sample response to Lars Eighner prompt

Lars Eighner's essay makes a provocative argument about the transience of material items. On one level, he is correct, for Americans do rely so heavily upon their material goods that we have become not only wasteful, but also unable to communicate with each other: a culture of people who "scavenge" cable television in search of something we have lost in between purchases. But Eighner's assumptions fail to consider the alternative—that if we somehow stopped buying items and filling Dumpsters we would be a society that would be better off. It is not materialism that stands in the way of self-reliance, but rather something more internal.

This template introduces the purpose

This template introduces a disagreement.

Eighner's pathos does establish credibility, especially as he cites "commonplace objects" that occupy Dumpsters. His selection of detail evokes the playthings of children and girls: stuffed animals, diaries, "shredded wedding books," love letters, and even a discarded needlework apparatus. By selecting more sensitive objects, Eighner effectively creates an almost nostalgic feel for these cast away items, and such a move suggests that what remains sensitive to him has lost its meaning to the previous owners. He correctly ascribes to college students a certain degree of wastefulness; these are children of privilege who can throw away a kit that is designed to create crafted decorative material, while Eighner is able to teach himself how to use the apparatus. The assumption here is that what the college students are learning—at least according to this image—is far less immediate and practical that what Eighner is able to teach himself, and therefore his message of self-reliance is initially conveyed.

This template connects technique (appeals) to purpose.

This template—an adverb—is a marker of evaluation.

This template signals an agreement.

Commentary

The major organizational pattern for the evaluation of an argument is to find the points where you agree and/or disagree with the author's assertion. You may choose to work your way down from the top, or you may look to organize your response based upon the areas that you agree or disagree with.

One clear focus of evaluation is to show your judgment, as seen in the choice of words that signify an opinion:

> . . . Eighner effectively creates an almost nostalgic feel

The adverb *effectively* communicates the writer's judgment or opinion.

You are encouraged to modify the templates to suit your own writing style. A template to introduce disagreement is:

> Though the argument is airtight with respect to _____, other parts have flaws.

The way this template appears in the text is:

> But Eighner's assumptions fail to consider the alternative—that if we somehow stopped buying items and filling Dumpsters we would be a society that would be better off.

Guided Practice

Step 4: *Application of templates*

You Try It Now it is your turn to enter the conversation. In your notebook, continue the evaluation of the excerpt by Lars Eighner by focusing on his argument about the animal life of Dumpsters. Return to your graphic organizer from Step 3 to assist you here. As you work your way down the text, determine the moves the writer is making, the effects of those moves on the writer's overall purpose, and where you find yourself if influenced by the argument.. Then, look at the catalogue of templates for evaluation of argument located on pages 25–27 to help you construct key sentences in your response.

Excerpt for Practice

30   In the area I know best I have never discovered vermin in the Dumpsters, but there are two kinds of kitty surprise. One is alley cats who I meet as they leap, claws first, out of Dumpsters. This is especially thrilling when I have Lizbeth in tow. The other kind of kitty surprise is a plastic garbage bag filled with some ponderous, amorphous mass. This always proves to be used cat litter.

35   City bees harvest doughnut glaze and this makes the Dumpster at the doughnut shop more interesting. My faith in the instinctive wisdom of animals is always shaken whenever I see Lizbeth attempt to catch a bee in her mouth, which she does wherever bees are present. Evidently some birds find Dumpsters profitable, for birdie surprise is almost as common as kitty surprise of the first kind. In hunting season all kinds of small game turn up in Dumpsters, some of it, sadly, not entirely dead. Curiously, summer and winter, maggots are uncommon.

45   The worst of the living and near-living hazards of the Dumpsters are the fire ants. The food they claim is not much of a loss, but they are vicious and aggressive. It is very easy to brush against some surface of the Dumpster and pick up half a dozen or more fire ants, usually in some sensitive area such as the underarm.

Write your response in your notebook and compare it with the following:

Continuation of sample response to Lars Eighner prompt

Almost anticipating his audience's outrage at scavenging through a Dumpster for his own personal gratification, Eighner acknowledges the "vermin" that occupy these places. Ranging from the "kitty surprise" to the "zillion fire ants," the author almost playfully acknowledges the unpredictable side of dumpster diving. That he's accompanied by his dog, Lizbeth, softens an otherwise repulsive scene, and Eighner himself seems to be able to laugh at himself when he notes

This template introduces an audience.

that all kinds of "small game" sadly, are not dead. Such understatement both anticipates and mitigates audience outrage; by confronting this more dire aspect, he successfully deemphasizes himself as the subject and effectively transitions into his argument on the transience of material items.

This adverb shows agreement.

And he is correct, for he establishes the context of a country littered with cities, and what he sees on a local scale is now a national phenomenon. We are a society that struggles to hold on to its "mental" values any longer than we do our material items. We often work in jobs where "the lowest common denominator" strips us of humanity, and we become automatons in a bureaucratic world. We think our only salve, argues Eighner, is somehow to escape from this world into materialism. And the greatest irony of all is that a homeless Dumpster diver like the author bears a stark similarity to a wealthy person: both have many possessions that they know will one day be discarded. And every time an item is discarded, the values that we invested with that item are also discarded.

This template brings in outside evidence to show agreement.

Commentary

Templates may or may not be complete sentences; note that in the first example, the template is added on to a fuller statement by the author.

The remainder of the evaluation appears below. Make note of those parts of the essay which you think incorporate templates for any aspect of rhetorical analysis.

Remainder of sample response to Lars Eighner prompt

Where Eighner's argument falls short, however, is the assumption that the absence of material goods somehow restores a deeper level of humanity. He writes: "Now I hardly pick up a thing without envisioning the time I will cast it aside. This I think is a healthy state of mind." By this logic, he would be obliged never to own a single item, or by extension, never to invest value in any item. And by further extension, all would live as Eighner does. Even if we were not Dumpster diving, would we never own books?

Further, the writer fails to account for the reasons why many of the personal items are in the Dumpsters to begin with. A shredded wedding book, for example, does not tell the whole story, any more than a discarded embroidery kit. Yes, there is wastefulness in our society, but to ascribe to the former owners a blanket statement about their living habits is an overgeneralization. What does the act of looking through other people's love letters say about him? Are we then to become a society of voyeurs? And the author's emotional appeals sugarcoat this work. By calling Dumpster diving "pleasant" outdoor work, he equates this work as if it were some kind of gardening, and he describes the "vermin" in whimsical tones, suggesting that they are playful companions.

His deepest flaw in the argument, however, comes from his claim that Americans' channel surfing is a function of mindlessness. He writes: "Yet in spite of the element of chance, scavenging more than most other pursuits tends to yield returns in some proportion to the effort and intelligence brought to bear." Those individuals whose work reflects their "effort and intelligence" do have the rewards of their own life, and it is not for Eighner to oversimplify the achievements of such individuals. If a psychiatrist, for example, chooses to surf cable television at the end of an arduous day, does that minimize his self-reliance? And where does the author acknowledge that his own livelihood comes at the expense of leftovers from others? If the society were to follow his dictum, then would he be out of a job?

Like Thoreau, Eighner's choices in life are to prove a point, and he succeeds in calling Americans to a greater awareness about the importance of taking materials for granted. But to take instances of trash found in various Dumpsters throughout a terrain, and then to deductively determine a truth that extends to all parts of our society is an equation fraught with error. To his credit, Eighner never takes himself too seriously, and because of this, his sympathy for us at the end does bear witness. Have we become so enmeshed in material goods that they now start to own us? Yes we have, but the solution is not to turn off the television.

Wrapping Up the Unit You have seen three different approaches to analyzing the rhetoric of essays and the templates that allow you to enter into a meaningful conversation on the pieces under consideration. Whether you work through the top-down analysis, analysis of technique, or evaluation of argument, you now have some strategies for producing thoughtful and effective responses to the work of writers who put pen to paper, or finger to keyboard, before you.

Argument

Portal 1

Finding the Portal

The Classical Model

Up until now, portals have been used to identify how you enter into a conversation as *both* a reading and a writing experience. You may also discover portals when the reading experience is farther removed—or even absent—from the writing experience, as is often the case when you write original argument.

Yes, your evidence may come from things you've read in the past, but here the analytical process has evolved into an evaluative one, whereby your task is to render an informed opinion. One of the most common entrances into argument is the presentation of the two sides of a debate, or the **classical model** of argumentation. Here, you present your opinion on a claim that often has two clear sides: for and against.

Agreeing with an assertion is simply that: you support the claim being made. To disagree is more complex, for there are parts of the assertion that you may support, but in general, you are against the claim being made. Qualifying is much closer to disagreeing, as you determine the boundaries within which the assertion is true or false.

A related task is to evaluate the pros and cons of a situation and then determine which side is more compelling. Here, your task is not only to present the two sides of an issue, but also to evaluate them and then determine the stronger side.

The portal using the classical model often reveals an understanding of both sides of a claim. Even if you fully agree or disagree with a claim, by acknowledging the other side—called a **concession**—you establish greater credibility as a writer.

The Reading Experience

Unlike the process of analysis, where the text precedes the writing, the process of argument represents an inversion, whereby you create the text, or argument; in effect, you use the skills of analysis and synthesis in the development of original argument. Original argument is an application of rhetorical analysis and synthesis to a new topic.

The classical argument often suggests that there is a right and wrong approach. Because you are often presented with two sides of an issue, you will find frequent occasions for the classical model: Are you for or against the Iraq war? Gay marriage? Abortion? Should schools have a dress code? Should freshmen get a full lunch period? The classical model makes the argument accessible by understanding that there are two sides to every issue. Is Gatsby great? Does *Romeo and Juliet* present true love? Your experiences with fiction and nonfiction may present many opportunities for this type of argument.

The challenge with any argument—but perhaps most evident with this portal—is that you must present an *informed* opinion. Determining whether you are for or against something may be an opinion, but being informed comes *before* forming an opinion. The temptation, however, is to formulate your opinion first, and then find information to back you up.

The Writing Experience

The task of writing an argument requires *evaluation*, the most difficult of all the thinking skills. At the heart of effective evaluation is *effective evidence*, or evidence that offers *convincing* support. Following are three questions to help you determine if your evidence is effective or simply adequate:

1. **Does the example address an audience outside of your immediate surroundings?**

2. **Does the example have a timeless, almost universal, quality?**

3. **Does the example lend itself to bigger, deeper questions?**

If you are able to answer "yes" to all three, your evidence will likely point to greater *complexity*, a quality that requires your reader to stop and think at a deeper level. Complexity involves linking your evidence to big ideas, relevant issues, and controversial questions. Evidence such as this provides a meaningful and provocative context for your discussion and will give your reader a sense that you are a thoughtful, accomplished writer.

PORTAL POINTS FOR CLASSICAL ARGUMENT:

When writing a classical argument, key points to consider are:
- understanding that every issue has at least two sides;
- the distinction between immediate and distant, or causal evidence;
- the value of contextualizing an argument.

To help you write a classical argument, examine the following templates. Think of these templates as not only a road map of what direction to take in your writing, but also as a useful vocabulary for this direction.

Templates For Classical Argument

Introducing the claim and the writer's position

These templates state your position and the overall purpose of your argument. They frequently appear in the introductory paragraph.

The claim asserts _____.

The author believes that _____.

To some, *X* is the case. But to the author, *Y* is true.

I fully agree/disagree with the position that _____.

_____ is true when it comes to _____,
but false when it comes to _____.

Concession

These templates allow you to recognize the opposition.

Admittedly, _____ is often the case.

There are those who believe *X*. They argue _____.

Contrary to popular belief, _____ is true under certain circumstances, which are . . .

Refutation

These templates allow you to refute the opposition, and they typically come after the concession.

Despite assertion *X*, one needs to consider how often *Y* is the case.

X is true under these conditions, but not always. Here's an example:

For those who believe *X*, do they consider *Y* as well?

In fact, _____.

Inductive Moves

These templates allow the essay to expand to more societal implications, or broader concerns.

Such is the case on an individual level. On a broader level,
_____ is also true.

One need look no farther than _____ to see how
often _____ is the case.

On a deeper level, one must consider _____.

Yet, _____ is really the case.

▼ Deductive Moves
These templates allow you to take a body of evidence and offer conclusions or main points.

Based on all this evidence, one can only conclude _____.

Given *X, Y, Z*, it is small wonder that _____.

Even _____.

▼ Parts of speech which show evaluation or judgment
These words allow you to show your own opinion on the subject, a requirement for effective argument.

Adverbs:	accurately	foolishly	naively
	perfectly	blithely	insightfully

Verbs:	fails	succeeds	broadens
	defeats	overrides	ignores

Adjectives:	supreme	faulty	cogent	correct
	illogical	successful	clear	
	effective	adequate	limited	

Prepositional phrases/ Interjections:

	in reality	perhaps	in fact

▼ Questioning assumptions
These templates allow you to explore potential gaps in logic.

Perhaps, then, the claim means _____.

This argument makes the assumption that _____.

To what extent is _____ true?

▼ Concluding with complexity
These templates allow your argument to broaden the conversation, as opposed to ending the conversation.

But when it comes to _____, _____ must be the case.

Looked at another way, one can consider that _____.

Review these templates frequently, so that you can utilize their forms and content for future argumentative essays in the classical style.

The Conversation Begins

A standard prompt often features these two tasks:

• **Note** a current claim on a meaningful issue, and **state** whether you agree with, disagree with, or qualify that claim.

To learn how to accomplish those tasks, complete the following steps.

Guided Practice

Step 1: *Examining the argument*

Prior to writing an argument, make certain that you understand the claim and then compile a significant body of evidence.

> In his autobiography *Living to Tell the Tale*, South American novelist Gabriel García Márquez states:
>
> > Life is not what one lived, but what one remembers
> > and how one remembers it in order to recount it.
>
> In a well-developed essay, state whether you agree with, disagree with, or qualify García Márquez's assertion, drawing upon appropriate evidence for support.

Guided Practice

Step 2: *Pre-writing*

Discourse Activities Prior to answering this prompt, respond to the following activities:

1. Paraphrase the assertion in your own words.

2. What examples support this assertion? Divide your evidence into the following categories:
    Observations
    Readings
    Experience

Use the criteria above to brainstorm your responses to this prompt.

3. What examples refute this assertion? Divide your evidence into the following categories:
    Observations
    Readings
    Experience

Use the criteria above to brainstorm your responses to this prompt.

4. Where do you stand on the issue? Why?

5. How will you anticipate and address objections or opposition to your point of view?

6. How are you going to organize your response? Choose the model(s) that you will utilize:
- listing examples
- providing a concession and refutation
- comparing and contrasting two sides
- moving inductively and/or deductively towards your conclusion

Outline your response in your notebook. Use the templates found on pages 39 and 40 in your outline.

Guided Practice

Step 3: *Writing and integrating templates*

Listening In Let's listen to how one voice may use the templates in a sample argument.

Sample response to García Márquez prompt

    To a storyteller, memory is everything, and when we recount our experiences to others, we do often create the truth as we see it. But to suggest that that memory trumps life experience assumes that somehow we fully comprehend life as we experience it when, in reality, it is only through time and reflection that we can come to grips with the full meaning of an event, and even then, more time and distance might change the meaning once again. Further, who among us—in telling a story—doesn't change his rendition when the audience changes? Can there be two versions of the same story? Gabriel García Márquez is correct in his claim that the role of memory and the way it's recounted matter most, but it is the experience of life itself that serves as the essential seeds of all.

    Life experience can permanently influence who we are, even if we are not fully aware of the full meaning of an experience. Some of these experiences are so strong within us, it is as if they happened just yesterday: a first paycheck, a favorite Halloween costume, taking a driver's exam test. Yet these experiences change in their significance over time. The actual amount of that paycheck becomes second to the feeling of being able to earn one's own money; what the actual costume was becomes second to the care and affection that went into our parents' making that costume; and what teenager doesn't retell the story of obtaining a driver's license with the glory of independence? García Márquez's assertion reveals the paradox of life experience: The greater the experience, the more difficult it is to fully grasp its meaning.

Identification of templates

Introducing the writer's own opinion

Introductory position with evaluation

Introduces the author's position on the claim

Commentary

Which comes first: your essay or the template? As you gain more experience with using templates, you'll discover that the answer can be either. You may know what you want to say and be looking for a template, or vocabulary, to help make that statement. But it's also possible to use the templates to help determine the organization of your argument.

For example, in the first two paragraphs above, the author of the argument looks to establish a more complex, nuanced position, so instead of having just one template to introduce his claim, the writer makes use of several, as seen here:

The first template relies upon two more basic templates:

> **1.** _____ is true when it comes to _____, but false when it comes to _____.

> **2.** Using an adjective that evaluates—in this case—*correct*.

The combination of these two templates provides this sentence:

> Gabriel García Márquez is correct in his claim that the role of memory and the way it's recounted matter most, but it is the experience of life itself that serves as the essential seeds of all.

The second template helps introduce the writer's position by noting a possible assumption; therefore, this suggests that you can reveal your position on several occasions, especially as your argument evolves.

The template used is:

> Perhaps, then, the claim means _____.

The actual sentence reads:

> Yet these experiences change in their significance over time.

The third template allows the writer of the argument to re-introduce his position, this time through the lens of the author. The template used is:

> The author believes that _____.

The actual sentence is:

García Márquez's assertion reveals the paradox of life experience: The greater the experience, the more difficult it is to fully grasp its meaning.

Guided Practice

Step 4: *Application of templates*

You Try It Up until now, you have been a listener. Now it is your turn to enter the conversation. In your notebooks, continue your response to the prompt above. Use your outline from Step 1, as well as the templates found on pages 39 and 40.

Now, compare your response and the templates used with the remainder of the original argument.

Remainder of sample response to García Márquez prompt

Identification of templates

In fact, by having to relate the experience to others, especially complicated experiences, we seek to create actual meaning by telling the story. Such was and is the case with 9/11, as Americans are still coming to grips with its impact on our society, and with each anniversary and retelling of the story, we gain fresh perspective on our international status. Our global economic crisis is another example; some refer to this as the Great Recession, but only with time and distance will we fully appreciate the economic impact of today's events, and it will be our memory of this time period that hopefully influences how we spend money in the future. Examples such as these fully support García Márquez's assertion.

An inductive move to broaden the discussion

Re-introduces claim; develops complexity

And there are even times where the retelling of the story will replace the actual experience, as if our memory itself dictated the terms of the experience. The award winning Israeli documentary *Waltz with Bashir* shows how memory of massacre is carried over from one generation to the next, severely influencing the ways in which future generations respond to violence. How often do teenagers speak with bravado about their athletic triumphs, despite their coaches or parents looking at the same moment with a more discerning eye?

García Márquez's assertion falls short, however, when it comes to those life experiences for which memory and its retelling have no place. Many World War II soldiers chose not to see *Saving Private Ryan* because it forced them to relive the graphic horrors of that time. Does a souvenir or photograph truly replace the experience? Hardly. This is why people enjoy returning to their favorite campgrounds or visiting favorite locations or eating the same favorite foods. Sometimes when we try to retell the experiences, we do ourselves a disservice by distorting the truth and putting ourselves in a vulnerable position. Perhaps it is a child's first refusal to admit that he stole a cookie from the cookie jar. Or the teenage driver who denied not coming to a complete stop. One can easily distort the experience to the detriment of ourselves and others. Even a character like Jay Gatsby was culpable of this, and his lies eventually proved to be his undoing.

Evaluation

Refutation

Deductive move

Perhaps, then, it is only those experiences that cause us pain for which we rely upon memory and our recounting of that experience in order to fully process the difficulty of the moment. But when it comes to those many moments of daily life that enrich us, then we have no choice but to return to the well of experience to nourish us once again.

Questioning an assumption

Concluding with complexity

Wrapping Up the Portal The approach demonstrated in this portal, that of classical argument, is effective when there are two clear sides to the argument, and you want to show that one of those sides is superior to the other. What do you do when there are more possibilities? The next portal gives you a strategy for dealing with that situation.

The Rogerian Model

While it is tempting to reduce arguments to two sides—for or against, pro versus con, right versus wrong—the reality is that most arguments have more than two sides. If the classical model initiates the conversation about how an issue has more than one side, the **Rogerian model** looks to see how you can find elements of truth within two distinct sides of an argument.

To find this Rogerian portal your approach must *present a willingness to entertain diversity*. The classical model is intended to polarize; the Rogerian model seeks to find common ground. As is the case with most controversies, there are parts where you agree AND disagree, so you make choices based on a combination of your beliefs and the writer's or speaker's message.

For instance, to say that one is for or against the war in Afghanistan is a potential oversimplification. Can one be against the war but in favor of fighting terrorists? Or can one be for the war, so long as all countries bear a similar burden of troop commitment? More local issues reveal a similar degree of nuance. If, for instance, we are debating the pros and cons of a school dress code, does the debate change when it comes to required religious attire? What about the psychological impacts of everyone wearing the same clothes? And how does the debate change again with many schools' newfound need to teach consumer education?

In fact, George Orwell, Ray Bradbury, William Golding, and other dystopian authors write of the dangers when we fail to question the arguments, even if we agree with much of what someone is saying.

To use a coloring book metaphor, the classical argument requires you to color inside the lines; the Rogerian argument allows you to color outside the lines. A common task would ask for you to consider **the extent to which an assertion is valid**. Note that this bears a clear resemblance to the language of **qualification** from the classical model, for you are determining the conditions or boundaries that apply to the prompt.

A related task asks you to **determine the most compelling point**. Often you will hear a longer argument, and you may find yourself agreeing with certain parts or disagreeing with others; as before, your own argument becomes a derivative—not just an agreement or disagreement—of someone else's position.

In general, when an argument is *grounded* in a context—that is, the conditions under which an argument is made have a clear connection to the argument itself—the appropriate portal is the Rogerian approach. You would not be inclined, for example, to agree with, disagree with, or qualify Lincoln's *Gettysburg Address,* given the Address's thoughtful relationship to a war-torn country. Nor would you be inclined to agree with, disagree with, or qualify an inauguration speech—again, a text that represents a specific time, place, and audience.

Yet, for a wartime address or an inauguration speech, there would be a much greater inclination to look for key areas that you support.

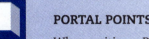

PORTAL POINTS FOR ROGERIAN ARGUMENT:

When writing a Rogerian argument, key points to consider are:
- those areas that you do find yourself agreeing with;
- the relevance that that argument has to your own life;
- the ways in which the argument attempts to find common ground between two sides.

To help you write a Rogerian argument, examine the following templates. Think of these templates as not only a road map of what direction to take in your writing, but also as a useful vocabulary for this direction.

Templates For Rogerian Argument

▼ Introduction of a position and accurate paraphrase of a writer's claim

These templates encourage you to establish an understanding of the position, or to demonstrate that you are a good listener.

The author believes that _____.

The author's most important point is _____.

The author's most compelling point is _____.

The argument is true up to the point that _____.

Such a position has validity when it comes to _____ but lacks validity when it comes to _____.

▼ Anticipating Oversimplification

These templates encourage you to entertain complexity.

Rather than believing _____, the author acknowledges _____.

At first glance, it appears that _____. However, _____.

It's true about _____. But the underlying issue is _____.

To say *X* is to believe that *X* equals *Y*.

▼ Synthesizing evidence through the syntax
These templates allow your syntax to combine ideas or examples effectively.

Given *X*, *Y*, and *Z* [nouns], which convey _____, the speaker proves _____.

The speaker believes that _____—often seen with *X*, *Y*, and *Z*—and therefore proves _____.

By joining *X* and *Y*, the author proves _____.

X, *Y*, *Z*: all reveal _____.

How can *X* and *Y* apply, but not *Z*?

▼ Establishing points of agreement
These templates permit you to choose which areas of the argument are valid.

_____ acts in the service of _____.

_____ exists in order to support the idea that _____.

By including _____ and _____, the author bridges the gap between _____.

A similar case can be found on a [smaller or comparative adjective] scale—a deductive move.

A similar case can be found on a [broader or comparative adjective] scale—an inductive move.

▼ Establishing points of disagreement
These templates permit you to choose which areas of the argument are not valid.

_____ is not the case.

There is little, if any, connection between _____.

True for *X*? Yes. And for *Y*? Of course. But for *Z*? Not exactly.

▼ Comparing and/or contrasting the two sides of the debate
These templates allow you to draw distinctions between different sides.

Paradoxically, _____.

One should not confuse _____ with _____.

Just because the author believes _____ does not mean he or she believes _____.

Just as *A* relates to *B*, so, too does *C* relate to *D* and *E* relate to *F*.

What *really* matters when it comes to _____ is how we view
_____.

The following words and phrases help create a linear essay, while still maintaining your own argument.

Transitions which show evaluation

Similarly   Hardly   Sadly   Frankly
Therefore

Transitions which withhold evaluation

Perhaps   Upon reexamination   Nonetheless

Review these templates frequently, so that you can utilize their forms and content for future essays with Rogerian arguments.

The Conversation Begins

A standard prompt often features these two tasks:

Note a current claim on a meaningful issue, and **determine** the extent to which this argument is valid.

OR

Note a current claim on a meaningful issue, and **determine** its most compelling point.

To accomplish both of these tasks, complete the following steps.

Guided Practice

Step 1: *Examining the argument*

Let's look at a sample prompt and see how templates may work to access the Rogerian model of argumentation.

In May 2009, President Barack Obama delivered the Commencement Address at the University of Notre Dame. Despite popular support for Obama in the 2008 General Election, many in this audience were concerned about how he would address the issue of abortion.

Read the following excerpt of the speech carefully. In a well-developed essay, determine Obama's most compelling point, and determine the extent to which that point is still valid. Use appropriate evidence for support.

Step 2: *Pre-writing*

Discourse Questions To help you begin writing about the text, answer the following questions:

1. What line(s) reveal an explicit position?

2. What line(s) reveal an implicit position?

3. Where do you agree with the writer or speaker? Make a list of those points.

4. Where do you question or disagree with the writer or speaker? Make another list of these points.

5. Paraphrase the central claim(s) of the assertion.

6. What assumptions do these claims make?

7. What is the effective evidence that supports AND/OR refutes a relationship between the assertion and the world?

Record your observations in a 4-column chart, such as the one represented below:

Areas you agree with	Evidence/explanation to support your agreement	Areas you disagree with	Evidence/explanation to support your disagreement

Step 3: *Interaction with sample text*

Listening In Read the text and the reader's annotations. In your notebook add your own annotations in preparation for answering the prompt.

Excerpt from *President Barack Obama's May 2009 Address*

Understand—I do not suggest that the debate surrounding abortion can or should go away. No matter how much we may want to fudge it—indeed, while we know that the views of most Americans on the subject are complex and even contradictory—the fact is that at some level, the views of the two camps are irreconcilable. Each side will continue to make its case to the public with passion and conviction. But surely we can do so without reducing those with differing views to caricature.

Open hearts. Open minds. Fair-minded words.

It's a way of life that has always been the Notre Dame tradition. Father Hesburgh has long spoken of this institution as both a lighthouse and a crossroads. The lighthouse that stands apart, shining with the wisdom of the Catholic tradition, while the crossroads is where "... differences of culture and religion and conviction can co-exist with friendship, civility, hospitality, and especially love." And I want to join him and Father Jenkins in saying how inspired I am by the maturity and responsibility with which this class has approached the debate surrounding today's ceremony.

This tradition of cooperation and understanding is one that I learned in my own life many years ago—also with the help of the Catholic Church.

I was not raised in a particularly religious household, but my mother instilled in me a sense of service and empathy that eventually led me to become a community organizer after I graduated college. A group of Catholic churches in Chicago helped fund an organization known as the Developing Communities Project, and we worked to lift up South Side neighborhoods that had been devastated when the local steel plant closed.

It was quite an eclectic crew. Catholic and Protestant churches. Jewish and African-American organizers. Working-class black and white and Hispanic residents. All of us with different experiences. All of us with different beliefs. But all of us learned to work side by side because all of us saw in these neighborhoods other human beings who needed our help—to find jobs and improve schools. We were bound together in the service of others.

Reader annotation

Wouldn't it be best if we could somehow reconcile these two views? Why can't there be some closure to this?

Does Obama really believe that the tradition of people working together will help solve our differences about abortion?

I agree. There are realities that cut across beliefs. Do these religious beliefs, however, also embrace the right to life?

And something else happened during the time I spent in those neighborhoods. Perhaps because the church folks I worked with were so welcoming and understanding; perhaps because they invited me to their services and sang with me from their hymnals; perhaps because I witnessed all of the good works their faith inspired them to perform, I found myself drawn—not just to work with the church, but to be in the church. It was through this service that I was brought to Christ.

At the time, Cardinal Joseph Bernardin was the Archbishop of Chicago. For those of you too young to have known him, he was a kind and good and wise man. A saintly man. I can still remember him speaking at one of the first organizing meetings I attended on the South Side. He stood as both a lighthouse and a crossroads—unafraid to speak his mind on moral issues ranging from poverty, AIDS, and abortion to the death penalty and nuclear war. And yet, he was congenial and gentle in his persuasion, always trying to bring people together, always trying to find common ground. Just before he died, a reporter asked Cardinal Bernardin about this approach to his ministry. And he said, "You can't really get on with preaching the Gospel until you've touched minds and hearts."

My heart and mind were touched by the words and deeds of the men and women I worked alongside with in Chicago. And I'd like to think that we touched the hearts and minds of the neighborhood families whose lives we helped change. For this, I believe, is our highest calling.

You are about to enter the next phase of your life at a time of great uncertainty. You will be called upon to help restore a free market that is also fair to all who are willing to work; to seek new sources of energy that can save our planet; to give future generations the same chance that you had to receive an extraordinary education. And whether as a person drawn to public service, or someone who simply insists on being an active citizen, you will be exposed to more opinions and ideas broadcast through more means of communications than have ever existed before. You will hear talking heads scream on cable, read blogs that claim definitive knowledge, and watch politicians pretend to know what they're talking about. Occasionally, you may also have the great fortune of seeing important issues debated by well-intentioned, brilliant minds. In fact, I suspect that many of you will be among those bright stars.

In this world of competing claims about what is right and what is true, have confidence in the values with which you've been raised and educated. Be unafraid to speak your mind when those values are at stake. Hold firm to your faith and allow it to guide you on your journey. Stand as a lighthouse.

These are interesting metaphors: lighthouse and crossroads, ones that serve cross purposes.

Obama is recasting controversial issues, such as AIDS or poverty, into a religious context.

He appeals to a higher calling through the spirit of collaboration, and this will help students through today's difficult times.

Obama is making an assumption—rightly or wrongly—that today's students will be more civic minded. He's encouraging them.

But remember too that the ultimate irony of faith is that it necessarily admits doubt. It is the belief in things not seen. It is beyond our capacity as human beings to know with certainty what God has planned for us or what He asks of us, and those of us who believe must trust that His wisdom is greater than our own.

This doubt should not push us away from our faith. But it should humble us. It should temper our passions, and cause us to be wary of self-righteousness. It should compel us to remain open, and curious, and eager to continue the moral and spiritual debate that began for so many of you within the walls of Notre Dame. And within our vast democracy, this doubt should remind us to persuade through reason, through an appeal whenever we can to universal rather than parochial principles, and most of all through an abiding example of good works, charity, kindness, and service that moves hearts and minds.

Is this a concession to what faith is? It appears that he's encouraging conviction on one hand, but also allowing for doubt or uncertainty. Is the religious context even still needed?

The use of the word "parochial" has a negative connotation here, and one wonders if he's implying that the private (or religious) institution may be too narrow minded.

Commentary

Your annotations on the speech above entered into a conversation with two other people: the speaker (Barack Obama) and one listener, whose annotations reflected his perspective. Given the highly controversial nature of abortion, however, there are *many* ways for you to enter into this conversation. Did you agree with the first listener? Did you disagree? Would it have been more helpful to respond first, and *then* see what another listener has to say?

What is most important is that your position is supportable through sound explanation and evidence. Most conversations worth having rarely have an answer key.

Guided Practice

Step 4: *Application of templates*

You Try It Up until now, you have been a listener. Now it is your turn to enter the conversation. Outline your response in your notebook. At what point in the outline will you seek that part of the argument that looks for areas of agreement? Of disagreement? Use your responses to the graphic organizer on page 50 as well as the templates that appear on pages 47–49 to assist you.

Read the following sample response to the prompt, along with the templates used.

> ### Sample response to Obama's Commencement Address prompt
>
> In his Commencement Address to Notre Dame students in 2009, Barack Obama's remarks about abortion provide a thoughtful reflection on how best to revisit this age-old debate. Rather than trying to defend or refute one side or the other, he notes that there are "irreconcilable differences," and in so doing, he presents the issue *not* as an either/or discussion, but rather as one that hinges on how we perceive

Identification of templates

Anticipating oversimplification

faith. The choice of the word faith (as opposed to religion) moves the debate away from pro-life or pro-choice into something more fluid, more conciliatory, more workable.

His most compelling point is that faith goes hand in hand with doubt. He begins by noting how faith allows us to serve as both a lighthouse and crossroads. By invoking leaders such as Cardinal Bernardin or Father Hesburgh—people instrumental in addressing social change at the community level—Obama notes that through faith we can take on difficult issues. A lighthouse is a beacon, something that lights the way for people to move out of the darkness. Often we are so saddled with the realities of difficult issues—such as poverty, AIDS, war—we need something more than just logic or tangible items to help us persevere.

Similarly, the image of a crossroads also allows an audience to understand complexity, as crossroads convey indecision and uncertainty, and we know that the decisions that are made at this time will chart our journey, or the journeys of those who surround us, forever. By coupling faith with these images of a lighthouse and crossroads, Obama redefines faith as something beyond the religious aspect into a more secular, utilitarian approach, yet one that also invites some of the intangible, moral, or spiritual connotations of faith.

Establishes position

Synthesis through dependent clause

Synthesis through interrupted syntax

Evaluation

Synthesis as an introductory clause

Commentary

Prior to identifying what is valid or not, an active member of a conversation demonstrates his or her ability to *listen*, and in so doing, establishes clear empathy with the debate. The first template used is:

> The author believes that _____.

Its more creative version appears above as:

> Rather than trying to defend or refute one side or the other, he notes that there are "irreconcilable differences."

The second template then provides you the opportunity to state your position. Note the effectiveness of first revealing your empathy *prior* to stating where you stand. The template used is:

> The author's most compelling point is _____.

And its creative version:

> His most compelling point is that faith goes hand in hand with doubt.

In addition to serving more spatial, thematic, or organizational goals of an essay, templates also provide you the opportunity to develop a mature prose style through sophisticated syntax. Templates to consider here:

> Given **X**, **Y**, and **Z** [nouns], which convey _____, the speaker proves _____.
> The speaker believes that _____—often seen with **X**, **Y**, and **Z**—and therefore proves _____.

And the actual response reads:

> By invoking leaders such as Cardinal Bernardin or Father Hesburgh—people instrumental in addressing social change at the community level—Obama notes that through faith we can take on difficult issues. A lighthouse is a beacon, something that lights the way for people to move out of the darkness. Often we are so saddled with the realities of difficult issues—such as poverty, AIDS, war—we need something more than just logic or tangible items to help us persevere.

Note that in both cases above, the synthesis occurs as an appositive—inserted into the actual text—in the service of presenting the writer's overall position.

Sometimes, a single word can serve two goals: to show your evaluation and to move the essay forward in a linear manner, so that it does not stay in the same place, or "tread water." The response reads:

> Similarly, the image of a crossroads also allows an audience to understand complexity.

The use of "similarly" above points to an area of agreement, while allowing the essay to address a deeper dimension of the speech—in this case, what the image of a crossroads signifies.

The remainder of the argument with templates for the Rogerian argument appears below. Read the essay and compare which templates the writer has used with those that appear on your outline.

Continuation of sample response to Obama's Commencement Address prompt

> Given the value of faith's role in bridging political or cultural divides, Obama's choice to bring in doubt at first appears to be a non-sequitur. Why would he encourage people to use their faith in the service of lighting the way through difficult times, only to entertain doubt? Obama notes that doubt "humbles" us and should "not push us away from our faith." Entertaining doubt as part of our moral or spiritual convictions almost seems as if Obama is contradicting himself, or simply playing both sides. Ultimately, the inclusion of doubt serves as

Synthesis as an introductory clause

Anticipating oversimplification

Establishing agreement

a concession—to counteract single-mindedness, even in the service of something moral or spiritual. Including doubt—a logical, rational phenomenon—with faith—a moral, spiritual phenomenon—bridges the gap between reason and passion, science and church, heart and mind.

Establishing agreement

At first glance, such a juxtaposition of doubt and faith addresses many aspects of our society. Consider the prevailing divides of our day: universal health care, government bailouts, gay marriage. Medicine, economy, education—all have advocates and proponents, and so often the debate rests upon how hardcore data stacks up in support of one side or the other. Scientific, legal, or economic approaches alone often struggle to arrive at solutions, largely because much of the controversy stems from intangible concerns. For example, much of the controversy around government bailouts of the mortgage or car industries rests upon the extent to which people believe that government should offer a helping hand. How can our government, for example, advocate health coverage for all, but at the same time deny the car industry more of a support? Does not this seem hypocritical? By taking current controversies with a moral aspect, the mixture of faith with doubt encourages us all to become beacons and roadmaps.

Synthesis as . . .
. . . direct object
. . . subject

. . . rhetorical question

The same relationship between faith and doubt also exists on a smaller scale. There are many issues in school where teenagers see themselves as for or against: a dress code, censorship of controversial material, community service. Yes, students will often fall into either camp, but both sides have value, and it's impossible to predict if going down one road is better or worse, for no "answer key" or hardcore data exists. But by looking at both the moral and logical aspects of the debate, students can learn to see what kinds of compromises will help chart a new direction. We have a reasonable defense of free speech, but we have a moral obligation to publish appropriate material; we can justify community service as a graduation requirement, but we must consider students' motivations when performing such service; rules to restrict the dress code must acknowledge students' feelings about personal appearance.

Deductive move

Synonyms to . . .

. . .synthesize
. . . reinforce

. . . expand

But to say that all issues merit the same balance is to say that controversy is controversy, no matter what. Such is not the case. There are issues to which Obama's "lighthouse and crossroads" metaphor struggle to apply, and these are ones where, quite frankly, less is at stake. Restricting the use of cell phones—a ubiquitous concern among today's teens—has little, if any, moral controversy at stake. Importing year-round schooling, omitting summer reading, giving extra-credit for volunteer work: all of these issues are immediate to students' lives, but they lack an emotional or moral legacy.

Anticipating oversimplification/
Establishing disagreement

Establishing disagreement

Today's headlines feature no shortage of similar concerns: imposing heavy fines for speeding through work zones; gaining political clout to get one's child into a prestigious college; bailing out the auto industry. Important and meaningful to many? Yes. Issues over which elections are won or lost? Absolutely. But ones on par with war, gay marriage, abortion? Not really. For even though we can try to reduce these weightier issues into a logical, reasoned discussion, we *must* acknowledge the emotional impact and, to quote Obama, our doubt.

Establishing disagreement

Therefore, Obama's message of entertaining doubt holds true for those issues which—paradoxically—are best addressed with doubt. But there are many debates in our country where doubt is, sadly, ignorance, and we too easily express our opinions—either for or against a point—for fear that we may somehow look foolish or uninformed. Perhaps, then, Obama addresses this ignorance unintentionally, for by forcing college graduates to look at the role that doubt plays in our convictions, they can begin to decipher which of those issues really *deserve* doubt, and which ones demand our pursuit of knowledge.

Contrasting with . . .

. . . adverbs

. . . nouns

Coming full circle

Wrapping Up the Portal It should be clear, after considering the approach discussed in this portal, that some issues require an admission of merit on both sides of the question. While to some this may look like avoiding taking a stand, in reality it calls for some intellectual and emotional maturity. For many writers and thinkers, this is the most satisfying kind of argument to engage in.

Finding the Portal

The Reading Experience

The Writing Experience

Competing Messages

While responding to a particular issue or message produces a certain type of argumentative style—classical or Rogerian—you sometimes find yourself negotiating more than one document at a time. Responding to multiple arguments or **competing messages** broadens your task, for you are weighing one message against the other.

Think of this as perhaps the most authentic representation of a conversation, for rather than speaking to one voice at a time, there are several voices; indeed, consider the most evocative moments of musicals, opera, or drama, where many voices appear simultaneously, sometimes overlapping each other. How you enter this conversation can be identified as the portal for competing messages, for by engaging several voices at once, you can pick and choose which arguments make the most sense to you.

This is often the case with the complexities of modern life. Jonathan Swift understood this many years ago when his well-known essay "A Modest Proposal" satirized the many proposals that had already been made to address the problem of Ireland's poverty. Fast-forward to today, and the ubiquity of proposals for any given issue can be overwhelming. The task, then, of negotiating competing messages also brings in a set of templates with which to develop original argument.

Note that this is *not* contrasting arguments, for such a task resembles the classical approach towards argument. Many election years feature rhetoric on both sides of the political aisle. Republicans might be for keeping Guantanamo Bay open; Democrats are against it. Democrats want dialogue with certain Middle East countries; Republicans oppose it.

Rather, the task of exploring competing messages is more frequent and more authentic in terms of how we respond to and create argument. For example, there are two (or more) versions of a plan for universal health care. Which one do you support? There are many ideas about how to reduce dependence on foreign oil. How do you know which one to listen to?

If you hear an aspect of analysis in your response to competing messages, you are correct. Sometimes you may be listening to nothing more than the word choices of an argument. Sometimes you may be carefully weighing the evidence that the message presents. The task, however, is *not* to identify which one is more persuasive, but rather to determine *your own* position in response to these competing messages.

The occasion for accessing this portal presents itself both implicitly and explicitly. Do you hear different homework policies from different teachers? Do the adults in your life emphasize a different approach towards physical fitness? Does your favorite restaurant provide more than one great bargain? If so, you are weighing arguments and making decisions in response to these competing messages.

Explicitly, you would use this portal when a writing task asks you to determine which of its messages is **more compelling** and the extent to which that message still holds true today.

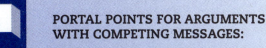

PORTAL POINTS FOR ARGUMENTS WITH COMPETING MESSAGES:

Key points to consider when writing an argument on competing messages are:

- listening to the prior arguments increases your empathy and credibility for your own argument;
- your own argument invites a comparison or contrast to these existing arguments;
- your own argument avoids an either/or approach towards identifying one who is "right" or "wrong."

To help you write an argument on competing messages, examine the following templates. Think of these templates as not only a road map of what direction to take in your writing, but also as a useful vocabulary for this direction.

Templates For Argument On Competing Messages

▼ Presenting similarities

These templates present your understanding of what other voices have in common.

In both cases, the writers state _____.

X and *Y* both say the same thing: _____.

How the messages are presented is also similar.

▼ Presenting differences

These templates present your understanding of how other voices differ.

Unlike *X*, who states _____, *Y* states _____.

_____, by contrast, reveals _____.

The manner in which these messages are presented differs.

▼ Concession/Refutation

These templates acknowledge your position against an existing position.

Initially, _____ is the case. But truly, _____ is the case.

X is the case, noted not for its _____, but for its _____.

We may not be _____, but we are certainly are _____.

▼ Evaluation

These words or phrases enable you to communicate your evaluation (judgment).

By adverbs:
eerily, accurately, naively, rarely, incessantly

By adjectives:
insensitive, sad, ironic, dog-eat-dog

By nouns:
corporate greed, billions of dollars, decades-long high

By verbs:
devouring

▼ Providing relevance

These templates encourage you to consider contemporary evidence to support your own case.

_____ makes the message more _____, as seen in America today, where *X* is the case.

[a seemingly unrelated concept]_____, as it were, reflects [a more relevant concept] _____.

_____, as also chronicled in the [literary work] _____.

If [statement from text] is _____, then [statement on today's society] _____ is/ is not the case.

Review these templates frequently, so that you can utilize their forms and content for future arguments on competing messages.

The Conversation Begins

A standard prompt often features these two tasks:

Determine how prior voices have weighed in on a given issue, and **present** your own argument relative to one or all of these voices.

To help you accomplish these tasks, complete the following steps.

Guided Practice

Step 1: *Reading the Texts.*

Examine how two different sources make competing arguments by starting with this sample question:

> Both of the following sources present an argument about eliminating poverty in a society. Read both sources carefully. In a well-organized essay, evaluate with appropriate evidence which of the two sources is more compelling.

Guided Practice

Step 2: *Pre-writing*

Discourse Questions After you have read the sources below, answer the following questions:

1. What is the main argument of source #1?

2. What assumptions, if any, is the argument making?

3. Where are there potential flaws in the argument?

4. What is particularly striking or noteworthy about the manner in which this argument is presented?

5. What is the main argument of source #2?

6. What assumptions, if any, is the argument making?

7. Where are there potential flaws in the argument?

8. What is particularly striking or noteworthy about the manner in which this argument is presented?

9. In what way(s) do the arguments resemble each other?

10. In what way(s) do the arguments differ from each other?

11. Stylistically, what are their similarities and/or differences?

12. Which one do you agree with more? Why?

Record your observations in the graphic organizer like the one below:

Voice #	Main message	Assumptions/gaps in logic	Noteworthy features of language
1			
2			
Etc.			

Step 3: *Writing and integrating templates [Part I]*

Read the following sources and accompanying annotation. Add your own annotations and responses to the discourse questions in your notebook.

Source #1: Excerpt from Jonathan Swift's "A Modest Proposal." This well-known satire parodied the failed attempts to solve Ireland's poverty.

Reader annotation

There is likewise another great advantage in my scheme, that it will prevent those voluntary abortions, and that horrid practice of women murdering their bastard children, alas! too frequent among us! sacrificing the poor innocent babes I doubt more to avoid the expense than the shame, which would move tears and pity in the most savage and inhuman breast.

The speaker appears to be compassionate and wants to save babies.

"I doubt" here means "I suspect."

The number of souls in this kingdom being usually reckoned one million and a half, of these I calculate there may be about two hundred thousand couples whose wives are breeders; from which number I subtract thirty thousand couples who are able to maintain their own children, although I apprehend there cannot be so many, under the present distresses of the kingdom; but this being granted, there will remain an hundred and seventy thousand breeders. I again subtract fifty thousand for those women who miscarry, or whose children die by accident or disease within the year. There only remains one hundred and twenty thousand children of poor parents annually born. The question therefore is, how this number shall be reared and provided for, which, as I have already said, under the present situation of affairs, is utterly impossible by all the methods hitherto proposed. For

The tone becomes more clinical; the focus on numbers and description of dire living conditions appears to be a setup for something.

we can neither employ them in handicraft or agriculture; we neither build houses (I mean in the country) nor cultivate land: they can very seldom pick up a livelihood by stealing, till they arrive at six years old, except where they are of towardly parts, although I confess they learn the rudiments much earlier, during which time, they can however be properly looked upon only as probationers, as I have been informed by a principal gentleman in the county of Cavan, who protested to me that he never knew above one or two instances under the age of six, even in a part of the kingdom so renowned for the quickest proficiency in that art.

I am assured by our merchants, that a boy or a girl before twelve years old is no salable commodity; and even when they come to this age they will not yield above three pounds, or three pounds and half-a-crown at most on the exchange; which cannot turn to account either to the parents or kingdom, the charge of nutriment and rags having been at least four times that value.

Is Swift really serious? "Salable commodity?" How is that better than abortion?

I shall now therefore humbly propose my own thoughts, which I hope will not be liable to the least objection.

I have been assured by a very knowing American of my acquaintance in London, that a young healthy child well nursed is at a year old a most delicious, nourishing, and wholesome food, whether stewed, roasted, baked, or boiled; and I make no doubt that it will equally serve in a fricassee or a ragout.

Is this the main argument? Eating kids?

I do therefore humbly offer it to public consideration that of the hundred and twenty thousand children already computed, twenty thousand may be reserved for breed, whereof only one-fourth part to be males; which is more than we allow to sheep, black cattle or swine; and my reason is, that these children are seldom the fruits of marriage, a circumstance not much regarded by our savages, therefore one male will be sufficient to serve four females. That the remaining hundred thousand may, at a year old, be offered in the sale to the persons of quality and fortune through the kingdom; always advising the mother to let them suck plentifully in the last month, so as to render them plump and fat for a good table. A child will make two dishes at an entertainment for friends; and when the family dines alone, the fore or hind quarter will make a reasonable dish, and seasoned with a little pepper or salt will be very good boiled on the fourth day, especially in winter.

This cold, calculating logic is indirect.

I have reckoned upon a medium that a child just born will weigh 12 pounds, and in a solar year, if tolerably nursed, increaseth to 28 pounds.

I grant this food will be somewhat dear, and therefore very proper for landlords, who, as they have already devoured most of the parents, seem to have the best title to the children.

Infant's flesh will be in season throughout the year, but more plentiful in March, and a little before and after; for we are told by a grave author, an eminent French physician, that fish being a prolific diet, there are more children born in Roman Catholic countries about nine months after Lent than at any other season; therefore, reckoning a year after Lent, the markets will be more glutted than usual, because the number of popish infants is at least three to one in this kingdom: and therefore it will have one other collateral advantage, by lessening the number of papists among us.

I have already computed the charge of nursing a beggar's child (in which list I reckon all cottagers, laborers, and four-fifths of the farmers) to be about two shillings per annum, rags included; and I believe no gentleman would repine to give ten shillings for the carcass of a good fat child, which, as I have said, will make four dishes of excellent nutritive meat, when he hath only some particular friend or his own family to dine with him. Thus the squire will learn to be a good landlord, and grow popular among his tenants; the mother will have eight shillings net profit, and be fit for work till she produces another child.

So the real targets of the satire begin to emerge: greedy landlords, restrictive religious practices, insensitive parents.

Those who are more thrifty (as I must confess the times require) may flay the carcass; the skin of which artificially dressed will make admirable gloves for ladies, and summer boots for fine gentlemen.

Even the language here lambasts the upper class—like a Dickens novel.

As to our city of Dublin, shambles may be appointed for this purpose in the most convenient parts of it, and butchers we may be assured will not be wanting; although I rather recommend buying the children alive, and dressing them hot from the knife, as we do roasting pigs.

Source #2: This cartoon from 2008 satirizes the government's current stimulus package as a way to curb one of America's worst recessions in history.

URL http://politicalhumor.about.com/od/economy/ig/Economic-Cartoons/Children-s-Debt.04hW.htm

· The first panel parodies common concerns about the present stimulus package.
· The listing of the burdens of the recession are, sadly, not exaggerated.
· The distorted donkey pokes fun at the Democratic party.
· The second panel is both absurd and real, in that the present stimulus plan will burden generations to come.
· The change in background and bubble shading over the two panels signals a shift in tone.
· The cartoon indirectly attacks the impracticality or impossibility of digging America out of its debts. The best America can do is make false promises and further exaggerate the problem.

Commentary

Your annotations above entered into a conversation with three other people: Jonathan Swfit, Walt Handelsman (the cartoonist) and one listener, whose annotations reflect his perspective. Given the highly problematic issue of poverty, however, there are *many* ways for you to enter into this conversation. With whom do you agree? Disagree? And what happens if this is a topic that you have little familiarity with? Do you feel qualified to enter into this conversation?

What is most important is that your position is supportable, through sound explanation and evidence. To reiterate, most conversations worth having rarely have an answer key.

Step 4: *Application of templates*

You Try It Up until now, you have been a listener. Now it is your turn to enter the conversation. Outline your response in a format like the one in the space below. At what point in the outline will you seek that part of the argument that looks for areas of agreement? Of disagreement? Use your responses to steps 2 and 3 above, as well as the templates that appear on pages 59 and 60 to assist you.

I.   Your Position

II.   Features of Argument #1

     A.   Content/Message

     B.   Style/ Rhetoric

III.   Features of Argument #2

     A.   Content/Message

     B.   Style/Rhetoric

IV.   Comparison of content

     A.   Reasons for preference

     B.   Evidence/support

V.   Comparison of style

     A. Reasons for preference

     B. Evidence/support

VI.   Exceptions

VII.   Conclusion

Step 5: *Writing and Integrating Templates [Part II]*

Listening In Read the following sample response to the prompt, along with the templates used.

Sample response to competing messages prompt

    Poverty seems to be a timeless curse of civilized society. What is equally timeless are the suggestions that experts have come up with to cure poverty. Jonathan Swift, writing in 1729, satirized all of the failed solutions for Ireland's poverty. Walt Handelsman, writing in 2009, satirized yet another solution for curing America's poverty. In both cases, the writers identify and criticize the plans to cure a nation's economic woes. And they both do so—indirectly—by pointing out that either country seems to be doing a very good job in destroying—or at least wanting to destroy—its children. These arguments share the belief—and the main message—that economic plans tend to be more self-serving for adults, rather than for the youngest members of our society.

    Initially, one may look at the cartoon and deem it more effective, given its overt statement of how generations to come will be saddled by debt; even the visual nature of the text is immediate and its message recognizable. But truly, it is Swift's timeless satire that remains more effective not for its style but for its substance—and that is its indirect attack on the causes of the poverty and an implicit statement of a cure. In short, Swift does more than identify that we are damaging our children's future; he offers a remedy of how to stop.

    Handelsman's satire indirectly exposes the weakness of the stimulus plan. By spending trillions of dollars on bailouts, a stimulus bill, the budget, we are incurring insuperable debt for future generations. The shift in shading and tone of the second panel—to a more serious, somber president—presents a sad irony to an often unspoken worry.

Right margin annotations:
Identification of templates

Similarity...
...in content

...in style

...in content

Concession...

...Refutation
Concession/Refutation

Evaluation...

...by adjective

Commentary

In situating yourself relative to existing voices—joining others, as it were—you achieve credibility by noting where the prior voices stand. The template that encourages this is:

> In both cases, the writers state _____.

Its creative application in the essay above is:

> <u>In both cases, the writers identify and criticize the plans to cure a nation's economic woes.</u> And they both do so—<u>indirectly</u>—by pointing out that ...

Note that a second template has also been used in the same sentence above, and that is looking at similarities in style. The template itself is:

How the messages are presented is also similar.

Note that the writer has in fact provided the actual similarity—"indirectly."

Because you must also position yourself in the conversation, you also look for templates that encourage you to provide your own evaluation. The actual language is:

Initially, one may look at the cartoon and deem it more effective, given its overt statement of how generations to come will be saddled by debt; even the visual nature of the text is immediate and its message recognizable. But truly, it is Swift's timeless satire…

Note how the words "initially" and "But truly" offer a concession—acknowledging what the cartoon states—and then a refutation—which support Swift's argument more fully.

Even the later adjective "sad" to modify "irony" reflects the writer's understanding of the purpose of the cartoon; in this case, the evaluation stays within one source, as opposed to two.

The remainder of the argument with templates for competing messages argument below. Read the essay and note which templates the writer has used. Then, compare the templates used in the sample response with the ones you used in your own response.

Remainder of response to competing messages prompt

Where will America get the money to bail itself out? It's common sense that one cannot keep spending to overcome debt. The indirect method of the artist's message—by pretending to be legitimate, even to the point of parodying a news conference—makes the difficult message more palatable, for so many people undoubtedly hope that by spending more money we will bail ourselves out. Anything but having to sacrifice. And critics of the current stimulus bill repeatedly point out that it is *not* the government's responsibility to bail out the problems that free-thinking and free-acting citizens of a capitalist society got themselves into.

Swift's message is even harsher, as we are doing more than saddling our children with debt. We are eating them, or we might as well be. The cold, hard, mathematical logic—coupled with the descriptive language of cooking or preparing food—presents the government as completely insensitive to the needs of its most helpless victims. That the speaker has been assured by a "knowing American" eerily foreshadows the avarice and greed of the United States.

Providing relevance

Evaluation…
…by adjective
…by adverb

Like Handelsman, Swift's writing is indirect, and by presenting this parody of an economic plan as real, he is—as it were—co-opting Handelsman's second panel. Swift's serious tone, enhanced by references to everyday aspects of Dublin life, make him sound believable, and it is small wonder that many of his readers thought he was serious. Even the acknowledgment of rich versus poor (as in referencing "those who are more thrifty") suggests a call to action that we should all be frugal, so as to subtly enhance his absurd argument about eating children. How rarely are Americans—by comparison—called upon to be frugal? Rather, isn't the message incessantly given today to spend, spend, spend?

But unlike the cartoon, Swift's satire more completely acknowledges the selfish behavior of the adults in everyday society, thereby acknowledging more of the burden of the blame. While Handelsman's cartoon flails at government ineptitude, the assumption there is that government just needs to get it right to fix the problems. Swift, by contrast, recognizes the perpetrators of such an erroneous, self-serving belief: the breeders, rich landlords, papists. Readers of Handelsman look at others; readers of Swift (ought to) look at themselves.

One look at contemporary America bears Swift out. The corporate greed of AIG is the perfect example; they took the bailout money and gave themselves bonuses. When American car companies asked for a bailout, they initially flew to Washington in corporate jets. Billions of dollars have been doled out for stimulus packages across the nation, but unemployment remains at decades-long highs, and in some places, like Michigan, unemployment is even higher in a post-stimulus economy.

If such crises did not impact the future as much, then our current economic crises would not invoke Swift's message. A glance at the future for youngsters today reveals a society that sadly resembles the dire straits of Swift's solution. Too many youngsters cannot escape the cycle of poverty from which they came, born back into a life of crime and drugs, as chronicled in Ron Suskind's nonfiction text *A Hope in the Unseen*, which lamented the burdens of Washington, D.C. ghetto schools. Those able to attend college and take advantage of higher education opportunities too often find themselves saddled with thousands of dollars in debt, and to make matters worse, are unable to find employment upon graduation. Perhaps in anticipation of the high stakes of our dog-eat-dog future, too many teenagers today burn themselves out with overly scheduled days, replete with high academic expectations and deep involvement with co-curriculars, often in vain pursuit of admission to so-called "desirable" institutions of higher learning. And what about those teenagers who have after school jobs to make ends meet?

Providing relevance

Evaluation by adverbs

Differences in...
...content

...content

Providing relevance with synthesized nouns (which evaluate)

Providing relevance

Providing relevance

Evaluation by verbs, synonyms

No, we are not eating our children, but we are devouring their childhood, and the messages today resemble those of a fading athlete struggling vainly to keep his star status: keep going, and you'll still be #1. Work harder, run faster, go for the biggest prize—like *The Great Gatsby's* final image of a boat against the current, constantly swimming upstream until there is nothing left. Our children have become adept at resembling us too well, and until we do a better job of looking at how the adults of our society have created this mess, we are not doing our children any favors in helping their futures.

Wrapping Up the Unit You have now seen three different kinds of argumentative essays, and have been given portals and templates to help you participate in conversations in all three types. Your responsibilities include determining which kind of situation you find yourself in and how much you know and need to know to make that participation fruitful.

Synthesis

Finding the Portal

The task of synthesis is virtually identical to the creation of original argument—with one significant exception: the use of credible current sources. When you use sources, you are entering a conversation that has preceded you, and you are offering your perspective, given your access to whatever parts of the conversation have already occurred. If, for example, you are joining the abortion debate in 2010, you have over 30 years' worth of legislation, editorials, and scientific research that will make your argument an *informed* one, more so than a person who was entering this conversation 15 or 20 years ago. Similarly, if you are engaging in a debate about whether or not to go to war in the Middle East, and you enter the conversation after September 11, 2001, then your ability to make cogent, relevant comments would be much greater. As David Jolliffe, former Chief Reader for the AP Language and Composition exam would often say, "Students need to know something about something." There are two fundamental ways to synthesize sources, both of which present varying degrees of assertiveness in your original argument.

Portal 1

Argumentative

The first portal is called the **argumentative synthesis**. Like the classical model of rhetoric, you are asked to agree with, disagree with, or qualify a position on a controversial issue. Such an approach presents a clear choice to you in terms of how you access the debate. Are you for or against the war in Iraq? For or against gay marriage? Bailing out the auto industry? Yes, you may have an opinion on one of these issues prior to reading how others have addressed this issue, and that's okay. But your task is to see how your own perspective interacts with others'.

As Gerald Graff and Kathy Birkenstein describe in their book, *They Say/I Say: Moves that Matter in Academic Writing*, it is important for you to *understand* where others are coming from, so that you can have a greater context for your own opinion.

Explanatory

The second portal can be introduced here, for it is strikingly similar to the argumentative one. This is called the **explanatory synthesis**. Like the Rogerian model of argument, you *withhold* making a decision for or against while you first consider key factors or concepts that allow you to make an informed decision. Thus, rather than deciding if you're for or against the war in Iraq, you determine what factors ought to be considered prior to making a final decision about the war. Perhaps you can see that by determining key factors or concepts—a process known as **rhetorical invention**—you are also making decisions, but the key word here is that you are more *restrained*.

At some levels, it is much more tempting to decide immediately if something is right or wrong. But issues that have staying power—ones that cannot nor will not be resolved in a generation or a lifetime—are typically complex and often require a reasoned, restrained discussion.

Remember, too, that these two portals balance each other. Note in the sample prompts below how they act as mirror images:

ARGUMENTATIVE STEM

> Synthesizing at least three of the sources, determine whether you agree with, disagree with, or qualify the notion that _____.

EXPLANATORY STEM

> Synthesizing at least three of the sources, determine what factors need to be considered prior to making a final decision on _____.

The Reading Experience

You'll notice that in both stems above the phrase "at least three" appears. Why is this? In the task of synthesizing, you are doing *one step more* than comparing or contrasting. All throughout your education you are comparing and contrasting, whether it's a True/False question, a Venn Diagram, or a Cause and Effect chart. You are used to the number "two" in your thinking. Synthesis broadens your thinking into a wider conversation, one that—like the Rogerian model—almost forces you to consider more than just two sides or reasons.

Does this make the explanatory model a more accurate one? Not at all, for even if you are writing an argument about why, for example, we should ban stem cell research, your *reasons* become the very factors or considerations that support your position.

The key word here is *current*. Unlike a great work of literature—for which a body of literary criticism has developed over many years—*current* conversations have far less certainty in terms of their place in the American psyche. Books like *The Great Gatsby*, for instance, will always have a place, but most readers of this novel have a pretty clear sense of what a conversation about it means in terms of America's past, present, or future. Not so with current debates, as there is simply less time, history, and written material to determine with certainty the significance of a particular issue for the present, or, for that matter, the future.

Hence the importance of choosing sources carefully. Unlike original argument—which often permits you to access your knowledge of history or personal experience—the synthesis task compels you to become students not just of a current issue, but also of *how* information is located and presented. You have an obligation to consider issues of credibility and context, as you explore the various locations of your sources. Is someone writing in a nationally acclaimed newspaper, like *The Washington Post*? And how would such an editorial compare, for instance, with a person's individual blog? Similarly, if someone uses satire to present a point—even if it's in a nationally recognized magazine—does that weigh the same as someone who uses a more objective tone in a local newspaper?

The Writing Experience

Whether your research provides reasons, factors, or concepts relevant to an issue, the task of synthesizing is more than just having sources speak to each other. You are also determining how the *ideas* merge into something greater. You do this all the time whenever you classify, and it is a human being's need for order that forces him or her always to classify or categorize. For example, how do you perceive AP classes at your school? What are the most important behaviors needed for success at homework? How do I define friendship?

When you rhetorically invent, you look for those categories, or concepts that develop from a more immediate to a more causal level. The following table provides a series of terms that illustrate how more immediate factors, concepts, reasons, or categories can develop into their larger-scale counterparts:

Immediate factor, concept, reason, or category, also known as context	Causal factor, concept, reason, or category, also known as context
Convenient	Economic
Practical	Political
Moral	Religious
Health	Medical or Scientific
Emotional	Humanitarian
Fairness	Military
Preference or Taste	General Health or Well Being

Given that synthesis is an argument using researched sources, the templates for the argument chapter are applicable to this chapter as well.

To help you write an argumentative or explanatory synthesis, examine the following templates. Think of these templates not only as a road map of what direction to take in your writing, but also as a useful vocabulary for this direction.

Templates for Argumentative or Explanatory Synthesis

▼ Stating your position

These templates introduce the writer's engagement in a current conversation.

Prior to making a decision about *X*, an agency must first consider _____ and ____.

I agree/disagree with the claim *X*, because of _____, ____, and _____.

▼ Rhetorical invention: factors, concepts, categories, reasons, context

These templates synthesize evidence into larger factors, reasons, or overall context.

One factor to consider is _____.

X says ____; *Y* says ____. The real issue is _____*factor Z*.

Looked at together, these studies point to _____.

How sources "speak" to each other
These templates are used for sources which agree with, disagree with, or qualify each other.

Agreement

Both sources X and Y agree that _____.

_____ is true, as supported by sources X and Y.

X asserts _____; Y agrees that _____.

Disagreement

Though source X argues _____, source Y argues the opposite _____.

X states _____. Conversely, Y argues_____.

Despite X and Y's support for _____, Z suggests that _____.

Qualification

With respect to _____*factor X*, this may be true. But when it comes to ____*factor Y*, questions arise.

_____ is true when it comes to _____*factor X*, but false when you consider _____*factor Y*.

Evaluating factors, reasons, concepts, categories, contexts
These templates are used for evaluation of sources, reasons, contexts.

Through questions

How fully does _____*factor X* take into account _____?

To what extent do reasons regarding _____ also include _____?

Does source X address _____*factor Y*?

Through comparison

On a deeper level, _____*factor X* carries greater weight than ____*factor Y*.

What matters less is _____. What matters more is _____.

Equally important is _____.

The cons do outweigh the pros when it comes to _____.

The most important factor to consider is _____.

▼ Anticipating opposing arguments

These templates are used for considering the arguments opposing your position.

Critics claim that ____. However, this is not the case, given that _____.

To the argument that _____, one can point to _____.

Clearly, evidence suggests _____, as seen in source *X* and *Y*. But do these sources consider _____?

▼ Using sources to enhance your own syntax

These templates are for integrating researched material into your own syntax.

According to _____ [author name], claim *X* is important.

Claim *X* is important, according to _____ [author name].

_____ [name #1] and _____ [name #2] agree that _____.

Various studies/claims suggest _____ ([name #1]; [name #2]).

X states _____; *Y* states _____; *Z* states _____.

▼ Using rhetorical questions to influence organization

These templates encourage the use of rhetorical questions as a transitional device.

To what extent is _____ really true?

How can we be sure that _____?

Is _____ truly accurate when stating *X*?

What other factors must be considered here?

Review these templates frequently, so that you can utilize their forms and content for future argumentative or explanatory syntheses.

The Conversation Begins

A standard prompt for the **argumentative synthesis** may read:

- Synthesizing at least 3 of the sources, take a position on whether you agree or disagree with topic *X*. Provide reasons for your position.

A standard prompt for the **explanatory synthesis** may read:

- Synthesizing at least 3 of the sources, determine what factors or issues need to be considered prior to making a decision about topic *X*.

To help you write an argumentative or explanatory synthesis, complete the following steps.

Step 1: *Reading the text*

Read the following question, as well as the accompanying sources.

The following prompt is presented in both its argumentative and explanatory versions identified above.

Guided Practice

BACKGROUND

The advent of biotechnology in sports has created a modern dilemma as disabled athletes can now compete with fully-abled athletes through the use of prosthetics, or artificial limbs. While no one disputes the trauma and courage associated with the use of a prosthetic, concerns in the sports world have arisen about the blurred boundaries between human anatomy and technology.

ASSIGNMENT

EXPLANATORY

Read the following sources carefully. In an essay that synthesizes at least three of the sources, determine the factors that a sports governing body must consider in allowing the use of prosthetics.

Or

ARGUMENTATIVE

Read the following sources carefully. In an essay that synthesizes at least three of the sources, take a position on whether or not athletes with prosthetics should be allowed in the same playing field as able-bodied competitors.

You may refer to the sources by name or as Source A, B, C, etc.

Source A (ESPN photograph)
Source B (Fermoso)
Source C (Stein)
Source D (Ad for The RHEO KNEE®)
Source E (Crouse)
Source F (Abbott)
Source G (IAAF)
Source H (TRS advertisement)
Source I (IPC)

Source A
Photograph from Sports Wesbite

URL: http://sports.espn.go.com/espnmag/story?id=3357051

This picture appeared on a well-known sports organization's website:

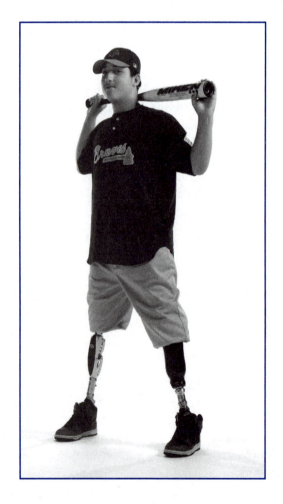

Source B
Fermoso, Jose. "Prosthetic Limb Research Could Lead to Bionic Athletes, Gadgets Controlled by the Brain." Wired, 2008.

URL: http://www.wired.com/gadgetlab/2008/07/prosthetic-limb

The following appeared in a technology blog entitled Gadget Lab: Hardware that Rocks Your World:

Scientists at the University of Pittsburgh recently succeeded in implanting sensors in the brain of a monkey, allowing it to move a mechanical arm with his thoughts. This is the latest breakthrough in the field of Neuroprosthetics, where implanted chips carry signals to
5   the remaining limbs of an amputee, guiding movement.

If the research holds, breakthroughs like these could lead to a reassessment of disabled people as "bionic" and fully able, and lead to a new era of mind-controlled gadgets.

Don't believe us? In fact, it's already happening.

10   Oscar Pistorius, a double amputee, uses carbon fiber-composite legs and doesn't define himself as disabled — he's already considered one of the fastest men in the world. The International Association of Athletics Federations (IAAF) agrees: When Pistorius requested to participate in the trials for the Beijing Olympics, he was flatly rejected.

15   Why? According to *Time*, "more energy is returned to [his] upper legs from his blades than from ankles and calf muscles and . . . uses less oxygen." He was too physically advanced to compete against "non-disabled" men.

It's true that his work ethic has a lot to do with his speed, but it's
20   the technology that allowed him to catch up with people with legs. And how can you measure the difference between a bionic person and a regular one in a competition of equals? You can't, at this moment in time.

There are other high-tech prosthetics that will push these bound-
25   aries further, like the C-Leg, and the Utah Arm (see list below). They include super-durable materials like titanium, as well as powerful chips that accurately replicate the lightning-fast reaction times of the brain.

And if the brain induces physical movement through electrical
30   currents and implants, it's not a big thought exercise to jump to mentally conducted gadgets. They're already lined with circuits and take precise orders. It's what they do. (We recently spotlighted a research that shows you can change tunes in your music players with your own eyes.)

35 So when you bear witness to the feats of the athletes at the Olympics next month, take a moment to imagine what a race would look like with bionic athletes. An Oscar Pistorius running alongside Tyson Gay, or Chris Paul dishing to his power forward, arms raised, finishing a dunk with a mechanical hand.

40 Here are three well-known prosthetic devices leading the way to the bionic era:

The C-Leg: This bio-gadget adjusts the flow of hydraulic fluid within a leg, through force sensors and a microprocessor rig that reads data at 50-times per second (similar to the one used on the 45 monkeys). The sensors detect any loading of the foot and ankle, and understand the exact angle of the knee joint, which is necessary for correct locomotion. It currently costs around $40,000.

The Utah Arm: This one is calibrated through the reaction times of muscles. Myoelectric signals are sent to electrodes placed on top of 50 the skin that control the chips implanted inside the arm, leading to precise movement. Price N/A.

The i-Limb: The artificial hand with the super small motors is the closest thing to Luke's hand in Star Wars. One of the best wrap-around mechanical prosthesis, it includes five individual digits also powered 55 by a two-input myoelectric signal. The individual fingers allow for the most dexterous, realistic replication. It's priced at $65,000.

Source C
Stein, Jeannine. "Faster, better, stronger? – Some high-tech prosthetics look as if they'd give athletes an advantage, but perception might not jibe with reality." Los Angeles Times, July 2007.

URL: http://articles.latimes.com/2007/jul/23/health/he-amputee23

The following appeared in a well-known newspaper:

With sleek, curved prosthetic legs that appear straight out of a sci-fi movie, sprinter Oscar Pistorius has been blazing across running tracks, leaving controversy in his wake. At issue is whether those carbon graphite appendages give the 20-year-old South African bilateral 5 amputee an advantage over able-bodied runners, an issue that has yet to be determined as he makes a bid for the 2008 Olympics in Beijing. No, say prosthetic manufacturers, other amputee athletes, and researchers. Maybe, says the International Association of Athletic Federations, the governing body of world track and field, which con-20 tinues to study the matter before making a ruling.

Although national Olympic committees ultimately select the competitors, technical rules in track and field are enforced by the IAAF. And one of its rules forbids "technical aids that give the competitor an advantage over someone not using them." As prosthetics improve and training techniques advance, such cases are likely to become more common. Even as prosthetic designers try to devise limbs that would be an improvement over biological limbs, many of today's amputees are determined to be as fit and competitive as possible. In doing so, they're going up against the fittest of able-bodied athletes, regardless of the odds.

Earlier this month, Pistorius placed seventh at a race in England, running the 400 meters before being disqualified for going outside his lane. But he had already garnered attention for holding world records in the Paralympics. Although he's not the first disabled athlete to compete against able-bodied athletes, he is the first bilateral amputee who may make the crossover. The prevailing sentiment among those who work with amputees is this: "I think he has a distinct disadvantage," says Hugh Herr, associate professor of media arts and sciences at the Massachusetts Institute of Technology. A double amputee himself, Herr is director of the school's Biomechatronics Group . "The prosthetic he's using is completely passive -- it's just a spring." A spring, he adds, that can't possibly compare with the force with which the human leg can propel a foot off the ground. "That comes from the muscles, and he has no muscles," Herr says. "He's just really fast." Amputee athletes must compensate for what they don't have—muscles, tendons, ligaments, joints, bones—things that even a state-of-the-art passive prosthetic can't re-create at this stage, researchers say. That compensation varies depending on whether a person is a single or double amputee, how much of the leg is left, and individual biomechanics. Pistorius was born without fibula, or calf bone, in either leg, and at 11 months his legs were amputated below the knee. He began competing in track at 17 and quickly began racking up medals in Paralympic events. He began racing against able-bodied athletes in 2005, coming in sixth in the South African Open Championships. He runs on the Cheetah foot manufactured by Ossur, an Icelandic prosthetic and brace manufacturer. Its J-shaped design, based on an actual cheetah foot, has been available since 2001. But as much as amputee runners favor the artificial running foot, it can't compare to the biological version, say scientists and researchers. In a 1987 study published in Archives of Physical Medical Rehabilitation, researchers evaluated the Flex-Foot, made by Ossur and similar to the Cheetah, against a human foot. Landing on a human foot in a running stride gave a 241 percent spring efficiency, or energy return, because of the contraction of the calf muscles. In comparison, the Flex-Foot

55 had an 82 percent spring efficiency. "It's the muscle that will actually help propel you," specifically the calf muscle, says Robert Gailey, associate professor in the University of Miami's department of physical therapy, and director of the Functional Outcomes Rehabilitation and Evaluation Laboratory at the Miami VA Medical Center. The bounce
60 that Pistorius and other amputee athletes have with the Cheetah is created not by actual springs but by the bending of the carbon graphite. An athlete still has to power his own legs, a force that in Pistorius' case comes from his hips.

Also, Pistorius' legs pound into his sockets with every stride, and
65 though suction helps keep them in place, Gailey points out, he still has to create stability as he makes contact with the ground. Stability issues and centrifugal forces may make it more difficult for him to maneuver around a curved track. Whereas able-bodied runners are fast out of the starting blocks, a lack of ankles and Achilles tendons
70 give Pistorius a far slower start. But the IAAF still has some questions to answer before it determines if Pistorius can compete (no date is set for that ruling). According to spokesman Nick Davies, the organization would like to measure the maximum amount of oxygen, in milliliters, that Pistorius' body uses in one minute, per kilogram of body
75 weight, and measure the mechanical efficiency of his running style using force plates, 3-D kinematics, and other techniques. All results would be compared with those of able-bodied runners. His running has already been filmed so that his stride length and speed over various parts of the track can be analyzed. Part of what may frustrate IAAF
80 officials is the lack of research done on amputee athletes. That, Gailey and others say, is due to the small pool of elite athletes available for study, and the fact that research money is used primarily to develop prosthetics to help people walk better.

That's changing. Today, bionics and robotics are two main areas
85 of prosthetic research.

Herr has developed the first powered, computer-controlled robotic ankle that allows a faster and more natural gait. It will be available to consumers in about a year, he says. He also developed Ossur's Rheo Knee, which contains a microprocessor that adapts to
90 changes in speed, load and terrain. At Northwestern University's Prosthetic Research Laboratory and Rehabilitation Engineering Research Program, director Steven Gard says his lab is working on a foot and ankle mechanism that will better adapt to changing terrains and walking speeds. Erik Schaffer, a certified prosthetist and owner of A
95 Step Ahead, a prosthetics and orthotics company in New York, says he's inspired by the athletes he works with to develop new and better prosthetics "as athletes push the boundaries."

But prostheses are still not as strong and powerful as biological limbs. Nor are they linked to the nervous system, Herr says, which would allow a person to "think and have the limb respond, so it behaves automatically in an appropriate way." Yet he and others working on improving prosthetics are sure that one day the devices will be more integrated with the human body. And here's where the debate about amputee versus able-bodied athletes gets even thornier: "Our goal is to design a running prosthetic that would actually give an amputee an advantage" over an able-bodied person, Herr says. The artificial leg would actually save energy as it propels someone along. So, as Pistorius narrows the gap between disabled and able-bodied athletes, technology could eventually split them apart again.

"If there are no constraints placed on what technology can be used," Herr says, "at some point there will be an advantage the amputee athlete has. In the future, Paralympic running times will be faster than the Olympics."

Source D
"The RHEO KNEE®"

URL: http://www.ossur.com/?PageID=2743

The following is an advertisement for a prosthetic:

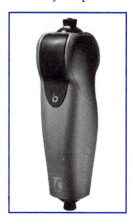

Imagine a prosthetic knee system so smart that it automatically adapts to an individual's walking style and environment, learning continuously and optimizing control over time.

The RHEO KNEE® is the world's first microprocessor swing and stance knee system to utilize the power of artificial intelligence. Capable of independent thought, it learns how the user walks, recognizing and responding immediately to changes in speed, load, and terrain.

The knee adapts to any situation, and not just within pre-set and limited parameters, enabling the individual to quickly regain confi-
10 dence in his or her ability to walk where and how they choose.

The RHEO KNEE is also available with a threaded top adapter (special order).This version of the RHEO KNEE is aimed for users with knee disarticulation or with long residual limbs.

Performance benefits:

15 **Continuous adaptation** - the knee system's highly developed artificial intelligence means that it is capable of thinking for itself. It continuously recognizes, learns, and responds to individual walking styles and keeps pace with changes in speed, load and terrain.

Natural and efficient motion - the high precision actuator technol-
20 ogy, which controls the knee's movements, produces an exceptionally smooth and fast response throughout every stage of the gait cycle. Unlike existing hydraulic systems, this response offers customized levels of resistance (knee flexion) as, and only when, the individual needs it. That's why walking effort is reduced to a minimum and motion is
25 much smoother and more natural.

Enhanced security - multiple safeguards are provided against inadvertent stance release, i.e. the knee is less likely to buckle at crucial moments. Disturbances in the walking path are recognized automatically and stance support instantly activated to protect the user from a
30 potential stumble and fall.

Simple and convenient - sophisticated technology that is easy to use—it doesn't come much better! The user-friendly "plug in and play" design ensures a straightforward set-up and calibration process with the minimum of fuss. The system is so efficient it only requires
35 a small battery that lasts up to 48 hours and that takes only two to four hours to recharge, at home or on the road. The battery can be switched off when not in use.

Source E
Crouse, Karen. "Phelps Rebounds Amid
Boycott Threat." NY Times *July, 2009.*

URL: http://www.nytimes.com/2009/07/30/sports/30swim.html

The following is a newspaper account of an international swimming competition:

ROME — The suit had to go. Michael Phelps made the decision Wednesday night after warming up for the final of the 200-meter butterfly at the swimming world championships.

All summer Phelps has been defending his decision to wear the

5 suit of his sponsor, Speedo, over other manufacturers' models made of less permeable, more buoyant material.

His loss Tuesday in the 200 freestyle to Paul Biedermann of Germany, who finished four seconds behind him in the Olympic final last year, was so untenable it prompted Phelps's coach, Bob Bowman, to 10 float the idea of Phelps's boycotting future international events until racing suits are returned to a state of being relatively equal.

Against that backdrop, Phelps slipped out of his Speedo full-body LZR Racer because it felt too tight and into a waist-to-ankle version of the same model. Then he went out and reached the one goal that 15 eluded him last year in his run of eight gold medals in Beijing. Phelps became the first man to swim the 200 butterfly in under 1 minute 52 seconds with a clocking of 1:51.51.

"That's about what I wanted to go a year ago," said Phelps, who won the gold in Beijing in 1:52.03. "To be able to do it with about six 20 months of training shows me that there's possibly still more in the tank."

Phelps's loyalty to a swimsuit that many people now consider inferior should not be too surprising. He has had the same coach, Bowman, since he was 12, the same prerace routine since he was 13, and 25 has stuck with the 200 butterfly, a backbreaking event, since making his first Olympic team in the event in 2000, at age 15.

Earlier this summer, after it became apparent that the new wave of swimsuits was building to a tsunami that would wipe out the record books, Bowman considered asking Phelps, 24, to try out one of the 30 new suits.

"Honestly, I had a temptation to put it on him in practice," Bowman said, "just so I would know for sure in my mind what the difference was. But then I thought no, because once he finds out it might just create a conflict."

35 Phelps, a 14-time Olympic champion, may be the Michael Schumacher of swimming. But his sport was never intended to be like Formula One racing, in which competitors hop from sponsor to sponsor in search of the fastest equipment.

Until recently, all suits were, more or less, created equal, and so 40 success in swimming was driven largely by that which could not be bought or bartered: talent, training, and tenacity.

The fabric of competition changed last year with the introduction of performance-enhancing suits containing polyurethane. Phelps's record was one of six global marks to fall on the fourth day of competi- 45 tion at the Foro Italico outdoor pool. In 32 events, 21 world records have fallen.

Source F
**Abbott, Jim. "How to Play Baseball and
Pitch With One Hand." 2009**

url: http://www.aboutonehandtyping.com/onehandedpitching.html

The following memoir was written by a Major League Baseball pitcher:

I was born without my right hand. I have never felt slighted. As a
kid I was pretty coordinated and growing up I loved sports. I learned
to play baseball like most kids, playing catch with my dad in the front
yard. The only difference was that we had to come up with a method to
5   throw and catch with the same hand. What we came up with, is basically what I continued to do my whole life.

I receive letters all the time asking me to describe how to switch
the glove from one hand to the other, in order to play baseball with just
one hand. Let me say right off the bat, there is no right way or wrong
10 way. I learned to switch the glove off and on with my dad when I was
4 years old and gradually made adjustments. Everybody has different
circumstances so it takes a little creative thinking and adjustability.
Try everything, find what seems most natural to you. Once you think
you've developed a method, just keep practicing and practicing and
15 practicing some more, until switching the glove off and on becomes
second nature, almost like tying your shoes.

I used to throw balls against the side of my family's house, pretending to be my favorite pitchers. When the balls bounced off the wall
I had to get my glove on incredibly fast if I didn't want to chase those
20 balls down the street all day! I would recommend a rubber coated ball
for this method.

As for holding a bat and hitting, it is a very similar process of finding what is the most natural motion for you. I always went with the
method that felt the most comfortable to me. For example, some peo-
25 ple said I should have hit right-handed, well, left-handed just seemed
more of a natural fit to me. I always wanted to incorporate both arms
as best I could. This way felt more balanced to me and more powerful. So I stuck with it. (I did get 2 hits in the majors, although I won't
mention my average!)

30 It is unquestionably a process of trial and error. Whatever you do
though, don't give up. Don't let anyone discourage you from believing
what you can accomplish. I have been so fortunate to meet so many
kids, all over the country, who devised ways of playing baseball that
you wouldn't imagine! They were just so determined to play and they
35 loved the game so much they came up with their own methods to help
them do it well. In the end, I guess that's my best advice to you—find

what it is in life that you love and go after it with all of your heart. I promise, if you have that passion, you will find a way to do what needs to be done. There is nothing that can hold you back!

Source G
International Association of Athletics Federation Rulesbook

URL: http://www.iaaf.org/news/kind=100/newsid=42384.html

The following is an excerpt from an international sports agency's rulebook:

IAAF Rule 144.2
Relates to the use of "technical aids" during competition

This rule prohibits: (e) Use of any technical device that incorporates springs, wheels, or any other element that provides the user with an advantage over another athlete not using such a device. (f) Use of any appliance that has the effect of increasing the dimension
5 of a piece of equipment beyond the permitted maximum in the Rules or that provides the user with an advantage which he would not have obtained using the equipment specified in the Rules.

It is important to underline that the IAAF does not have, nor contemplate, a ban on prosthetic limbs, but rather technical aids.
10 The aim of the rule change is not an attempt to prevent disabled athletes from using any artificial limbs or competing against able-bodied athletes if they are good enough to do so. For this reason, the IAAF is now compiling research on the technical qualities of prosthetics.

Source H
TRS Advertisement, 2009.

URL: http://www.oandp.com/products/trs/sports-recreation/swimming.asp

The following is an advertisement from a sports and recreational technology provider:

Freestyle Swimming Td. / Swim Fin Kit
* Direct Purchase Available *

The Freestyle Swimming Td. is a recreational accessory designed to be used with a custom swimming prosthesis for those interested in high performance or competitive swimming capability. The design, which mimics a folding wing, reduces resistance during stroke recov-
5 ery but flares open to provide maximum resistance during the power

stroke. The device can be rotated to optimize various swimming strokes and styles. The wings can be fixed in a flared position for treading water and water aerobic exercise. The Freestyle comes in an adult
10   size but can be easily modified down to conform to smaller hand displacements using standard shop equipment such as band or jig saws and belt sanders. (3.4 ounces, 6 inches long x 5.5 inches wide). 1/2 inch diameter, threaded stainless stud fits all standard body-powered, mechanical prosthetic wrists. No cable is required.

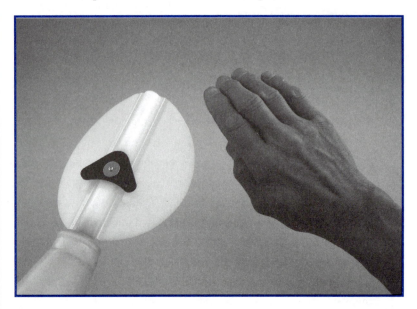

Source I
International Paralympic Committee Website

URL: http://www.paralympic.org/release/Main_Sections_Menu/Sports/

The following is a list of Paralympic events:

Sports

The International Paralympic Committee (IPC) is the global governing body of the Paralympic Movement. The IPC organizes the
5   Summer and Winter Paralympic Games, and serves as the International Federation for nine (9) sports, for which it supervises and coordinates the World Championships and other competitions.

Sports Governance

The governance of 26 sports (20 Paralympic Summer sports, 5 Paralympic Winter Sports, 1 Non-Paralympic sport) falls under the
10   responsibility of different bodies:

IPC Sports

Alpine Skiing

Athletics

Biathlon

15   Cross-Country Skiing

Ice Sledge Hockey

Powerlifting

Shooting

Swimming

20   Wheelchair Dance Sport (Non-Paralympic sport)

IOSD Sports

*Governed by the Cerebral Palsy International Sports and
        Recreation Association (CPISRA)*

Boccia

25   Football 7-a-side

Governed by the International Blind Sports Federation (IBSA)

Football 5-a-side

Goalball

Judo

30   *Governed by the International Wheelchair and Amputee Sports
        Federation (IWAS)*

Wheelchair Fencing

Wheelchair Rugby

IF Sports

35   *Governed by International Federations (IF)*

Archery (International Archery Federation)

Cycling (International Cycling Federation)

Equestrian (International Equestrian Federation)

Rowing (International Rowing Federation)

40   Sailing (International Foundation for Disabled Sailing)

Table Tennis (International Table Tennis Federation)

Volleyball (Sitting) (World Organization for Volleyball for
        Disabled)

Wheelchair Basketball (International Wheelchair Basketball
45   Federation)

Wheelchair Curling (World Curling Federation)

Wheelchair Tennis (International Tennis Federation)

Guided
Practice

Step 2: *Pre-writing*

Prior to answering the question, complete the two discourse activities that will help you write a more developed response.

Discourse Questions For each source, answer the following questions. Record your observations in your notebook.

1. What is the central claim for the source? Find one line that comes closest to this claim. Can this source say something completely different, depending upon the viewer or reader? Explain.

2. What assumptions does this source make?

3. How does this source agree with, disagree with, or relate to at least one other source?

4. How does this source help you answer the prompt?

5. What gives this source credibility? How does the credibility of this source compare with that of the other sources?

Discourse Activity Rhetorical invention. In the space below, find at least four different pairings of sources. Explain how or why these sources speak to each other. Then, determine a word or phrase that establishes the factor, concept, reason, category, or context that these sources help create:

Source Pairing	How these sources speak to each other	Factor, concept, reason, category, or context
#1		
#2		
#3		
#4		

Guided
Practice

Step 3: *Writing and integrating templates*

You Try It Outline your response. Use the following table to organize your response. Incorporate templates where noted. You can see how the argumentative and explanatory outlines mirror each other.

Argumentative Outline	Explanatory Outline

I. Position with Reasons
Incorporate template
 	
II. Counter Arguments (Concession)
Incorporate template
    A. Reason, factor, concept, category
      1. Source __
      2. Source __
 	
Incorporate template
    B. Reason, factor, concept, category
      1. Source __
      2. Source __
 	
III. Own Arguments (Refutation)
Incorporate template
    A. Reason, factor, concept, category
      1. Source __
      2. Source __
 	
Incorporate template
    B. Reason, factor, concept, category
      1. Source __
      2. Source __
 	
IV. Qualifiers
Incorporate template
    A. Reason, factor, concept, category
      1. Source __
      2. Source __
 	
Incorporate template
    B. Reason, factor, concept, category
      1. Source __
      2. Source __
 	
V. Conclusion
Incorporate template
    A. Synthesis of reasons, factors, etc.
 	
True or False? A source can appear in more than one place in your essay.
 	
TRUE!
 	
True or False? The above model requires a 5-paragraph format.
 	
FALSE!
	I. Reasons as your Position
	Incorporate template
	
	II. Reason, Concept, Factor, Category #1
	Incorporate template
	    A. Source ___
	    B. Source ___
	    C. Evaluative statement/ Incorporate
	       template
	
	III. Reason, Concept, Factor, Category #2
	Incorporate template
	    A. Source ___
	    B. Source ____
	    C. Evaluative statement/ Incorporate
	       template
	
	IV. Reason, Concept, Factor, Category #3
	Incorporate template
	    A. Source ___
	    B. Source ___
	    C. Evaluative statement/ Incorporate
	       template
	
	V. Reason, Concept, Factor, Category #4
	Incorporate template
	    A. Source ___
	    B. Source ____
	    C. Evaluative statement/ Incorporate
	template
	
	VI. Conclusion
	Incorporate template
	    Synthesis of evaluative statements
	
	True or False? It matters what order the reasons or categories appear. The order in which you present your factors reveals what's important (to you) in terms of how you lay out this debate.
	
	TRUE!
	
	True or False? The explanatory approach means you withhold final agreement or disagreement.
	
	FALSE!

Use a separate sheet of paper for your outline.

Step 4: *Writing and integrating templates (Part I)*

Listening In Now, read through two sample responses to the question. As you read, pay attention to how these two responses are similar and different. Highlighted statements represent the use of templates. Compare their use with the templates you identified in your outline.

Argumentative Approach	Explanatory Approach
While there is no question that we should applaud the courage of individuals who have bravely pursued athletic competition in the face of having lost a limb or suffered severe physical disability, allowing the use of a prosthetic in formal sports competition fundamentally changes the purpose of competition, and it takes an already uneven playing field and makes it even worse. The sports field is the one place that pits most purely pits one human being against another, and athletes have complete control over their abilities to perform. The achievements of a Michael Phelps or Tyson Gay are remarkable for their training and dedication, and they deserve not only adulation from us, but also our inspiration, especially as we look to explore our own physical capacities. Technology's development to allow some semblance of "normalcy" goes too far when it enters into the sports arena, as the prosthetic takes away the competitive purity of an athletic event.	With Oscar Pistorius outracing professional athletes—with two prosthetic legs—the debate speeds forward as to whether or not such differently-abled athletes deserve the same access to the playing fields as regularly-abled athletes. Whether it is a basketball court, swimming pool, or track, these arenas face an encroachment of technological devices that serve to enhance the athletic performance. Football helmets today feature protective visors; swimsuits have more buoyant material; tennis racquets use a lighter, more durable string; running shoes become lighter and sleeker. At what point, however, does technology take away the human element? Is the prosthetically enhanced athlete a sign of this technological encroachment—just the next step in creating fairer, purer competition? Or does the prosthetic cross a line, somehow taking away human dedication and perseverance to excellence in sport? Prior to determining whether or not to allow the differently-abled athlete to use a prosthetic on the same playing field, a sports governing agency must consider issues related to fairness, health, and democracy.

Commentary

The introduction of either mode of synthesis features a statement of the writer's position. The templates (italicized below) provided for this move and the accompanying applications of those templates are:

*Prior to making a decision about **X**, an agency must first consider _____ and _____.*

Prior to determining whether or not to allow the differently-abled athlete to use a prosthetic on the same playing field, a sports governing agency must consider issues related to fairness, health, and democracy.

*I agree/disagree with the claim **X**, because of _____, _____, and _____.*

Technology's development to allow some semblance of "normalcy" goes too far when it enters into the sports arena, as the prosthetic takes away the competitive purity of an athletic event.

Note that in the latter example, the omission of the first person – "I agree/disagree"—reflects a more mature entrance into a conversation, a move which identifies your awareness that this is an issue that has preceded your involvement.

Continuation of Argumentative Approach	Continuation of Explanatory Approach
Yes, there are many factors which would support the inclusion of differently- abled athletes into the arena, not the least of which is *fairness*. If someone has suffered extreme trauma and is willing to work harder to compete, as Jose Fermoso describes in his review of Oscar Pistorius, then he should be allowed to compete. "Pistorius doesn't define himself as disabled," writes Fermoso, whose story complements ESPN's image of an optimistic young man with prosthetics, smiling hopefully at the camera, as if to question whether or not the viewer would deny him a chance to play baseball just because he has no legs (2008). Such an appeal to sympathy and an appeal to our inspirations make us human, for who among us would look at an amputee and deny him access to athletic competition? An equally important factor is the health reason. If anything, amputees or disabled individuals need that athletic	One key area to consider is fairness. Proponents like Oscar Pistorius question how a sports governing body would deny an athlete doing essentially the same thing, just with two artificial legs. Jose Fermoso describes the tumult surrounding Pistorius' achievement, despite the athlete's outstanding "work ethic," and Jeannine Stein describes how current prosthetics cannot compare with natural limbs; both writers agree that the use of prosthetics changes the playing field and causes great concern to athletes (2008;2007). Nor are these limbs linked to the nervous system, Herr says, which would allow a person to "think and have the limb respond, so it behaves automatically in an appropriate way," as writes Stein, whose comments suggest an almost paranoid insensitivity on the part of those who would deny access (2007). Conversely, Stein's argument is addressed almost head on by nearly

outlet for physical and emotional health. The exhaustive line up of sports for the Paralympic Games features games like boccia or wheelchair fencing, games specifically designed to allow differently-abled people to participate (2009). And for the swimmer without a hand, the TRS advertisement is just the latest invention to allow human desire to transcend corporal limits (2009).

And even a third reason to keep such athletes on the same playing field is a political one. Do we wish to create a sub-class of citizen-athletes? By denying access to a professional sports arena, how different are we from those who discriminate based upon other physical features? Jim Abbott, a one-armed professional pitcher, even writes: "Whatever you do though, don't give up" (2009). The human spirit must reign supreme. And the Rheo Knee—another technological breakthrough—features "continuous adaptation," so that the argument against an unfair advantage—as stated against the Pistorius example—is an empty one, given that technology is becoming more and more "natural" (2009).

opposite concerns, as there will come a point—if we are not already there—where technology will permeate even *invisible*, not just visible, aspects of the athletes. Both Stein and Fermoso allude to neurological implants that influence how we direct our bodies to perform athletically. Michael Phelps's concerns over today's swimsuits straddle two sides of the debate—the pure athlete vs. the technologically enhanced one; hence, they are a kind of middle ground between those visible and invisible influences of technology. On the surface, the swimsuits appear the same, but the lighter, more buoyant material gives an alleged advantage to athletes. Or as Karen Crouse suggests in her report on Phelps, such devices allow athletes to view competition as something other than just human spirit (2009). Perhaps this is one reason for the proliferation of steroids in key sports.

Commentary

The highlighted sentences above represent three distinct templates: (1) to establish rhetorical invention; (2) to evaluate factors or context; and (3) to synthesize sources.

1. The templates to establish rhetorical invention are italicized, followed by the actual sentences and analysis:

   One factor to consider is _____.

   X says ____; Y says ____. The real issue is _____factor Z.

   Looked at together, these studies point to _____.

   - And even a third reason to keep such athletes on the same playing field is a political one.
   - An equally important factor is the health reason.
   - One key area to consider is fairness.
   - Yes, there are many factors which would support the inclusion of differently-abled athletes into the arena, not the least of which is *fairness*.

2. Some templates to evaluate factors or contexts are italicized below:

*On a deeper level, _____ **factor X** carries greater weight than ____ **factor Y**.*

What matters less is _____. What matters more is _____.

Equally important is _____.

A review of the application of these templates reveals that some sentences fulfill two purposes—not only to establish rhetorical invention but also to evaluate. When you determine the organization of your essay, consider why the most or least important factors/reasons/contexts/categories belong where they do. By creating this order, you begin the process of evaluation, where you weigh one factor against another.

Consider once more these two sentences, the first from the argumentative response:

> An equally important factor is the health reason.

Here, the writer's use of the word "equally" signals his evaluation that a particular factor—health, in this case—bears as much importance as the factor that has preceded it.

And this sentence from the explanatory response:

> Conversely, Stein's argument is addressed almost head on by nearly opposite concerns, as there will come a point—if we are not already there—where technology will permeate even *invisible*, not just visible, aspects of the athletes.

Here, the writer anticipates the concerns about fairness by establishing yet a new context: visible or invisible influences upon sports performance. In the previous section, Stein had dismissed the issue of fairness, claiming that prosthetics could never be as strong as biological limbs. Yet the writer's decision to *follow* this claim with an opposite point of view reveals his evaluation over the incompleteness of Stein's claim.

Some templates which features sources speaking to each other are italicized below:

> ### Agreement
>
> *Both sources **X** and **Y** agree that _____.*
>
> *_____ is true, as supported by sources **X** and **Y**.*
>
> *__X__ asserts _____; __Y__ agrees that _____.*
>
> "Pistorius doesn't define himself as disabled," writes Fermoso, whose story complements ESPN's image of an optimistic young man with prosthetics, smiling hopefully at the camera…

Note that in the above example—from the argumentative response—the word "complements" acts as a synonym for "agrees with."

> Jose Fermoso describes the tumult surrounding Pistorius' achievement, despite the athlete's outstanding "work ethic," and Jeannine Stein describes how current prosthetics cannot compare with natural limbs; both writers agree that the use of prosthetics changes the playing field and causes great concern to athletes.

Note that in the above example, the writer has provided a brief summary in order to establish the agreement. In this way, the writer also provides clearer attribution to what the sources state.

Guided Practice

Step 5: *Application of templates*

You Try It Up until now, you have been a listener. Now it is your turn to enter the conversation. Continue in your notebook with *either* an explanatory or argumentative response. To assist you in your synthesis, use your outline that you previously completed, as well as the templates for this section. These appear on pages 74–76. Then compare your response with the one given.

Step 6: *Writing and integrating templates (Part II)*

Listening In Continue listening to the following two responses. Underline those portions of the text which you think make use of templates.

Remainder of Argumentative Approach	Remainder of Explanatory Approach
Despite the reasons for inclusion, they are less compelling than the reasons to deny access for prosthetically enhanced athletes. First and foremost is fairness. The IAFF's rule book clearly states that "no technical aid" is permitted on the playing field, and Fermoso himself describes how the amputee's fake legs use less oxygen and therefore give him greater energy (2009; 2008). The TRS fin, while admirable, provides greater pull against the water than the human hand, and provides an equally unfair advantage. Even Karen Crouse agrees, commenting on how Michael Phelps's example transcends the use of technology to restore our beliefs that at the core of athletic excellence is something other than technology (2009). An even greater reason is the technological blurring between technology and sport. New inventions are made all the time to help out performance. According to Crouse, Michael Phelps wants swim suits to return "to a state of being relatively equal" (2009). Sports companies are making lighter shoes, more balanced golf clubs, more durable basketballs. Technology is getting dangerously close to moving from enhancing human performance to enabling human performance. Even the TRS swim fin states the device is suitable "for those interested in high performance or competitive swimming capability" (2009). It is the nature of the sports manufacturing industry to pursue faster, bigger, better, and we must remain vigilant about where the boundaries are. Finally, the sociological concerns about a sub-class of citizen-athletes are unfounded. Consider that organizations	Health is an equally important issue to consider. Do we want a group of differently-abled citizens to live unhealthy lives? Absolutely not. ESPN's photography of an ordinary looking man—from the waist up—appeals to our sympathy and compassion, not mention our inspiration, to allow those with prosthetics to compete (2009). Who among us would be so callous as to say that such an individual has an unfair advantage? Do we not instead cheer for him who has surmounted the odds? The Rheo Knee represents only the latest in breakthroughs that give athletes access. "Unlike existing hydraulic systems, this response offers customized levels of resistance (knee flexion) as, and only when, the individual needs it. That's why walking effort is reduced to a minimum and motion is much smoother and more natural," says the advertisement (2009). And just how many athletes like Pistorius ever truly challenge for supremacy? Has there ever been a champion—in a regular sport—who is differently-abled? There is a difference, one may argue, between athletic participation and advanced levels of competition. Allowing a prosthetically enabled athlete to participate on a playing field does not assume that he or she gets to compete at the highest level, where governing bodies must abide by strict rules to ensure fairness. Much in the way major league baseball has had to come to grips with steroid use, each governing body must determine the extent to which a "technical aid" unfairly influences performance (IAAF rulebook). At the core of this debate, however, is the concern that exclusion flies in the face of democratic values. By not allowing access to differently-abled athletes, critics

like the Paralympics are designed expressly for differently-abled athletes, even to the point of creating sports exclusively for such differently-abled athletes (2009). Since not everyone can participate in wheelchair fencing, then why should everyone participate in everyday fencing? Admittedly, moving into the world of "professional athletes" would resemble a minor league baseball player making it into the big leagues, but that's more a reflection on our own society's mania for competition and achievement, irrespective of what best suits the needs of a differently-abled athlete. Does a Paralympics Gold Medalist somehow feel cheated because she didn't compete in the real Olympics?

That sport brings out the best in human dedication and perseverance is undeniable, and we are correct to encourage all individuals—regardless of ability—to compete at their highest level. But to balance the realities of the playing field against the much greater realities of a democracy is unfair to the world of sports. Just as not everyone will be differently-abled, not everyone will be an athletic competitor, and for those areas where people choose to participate, we have the right to determine who gets in and who doesn't.

argue, we are creating a sub-class of citizens no different from victims of other forms of discrimination. But this is why the Paralympic Games have enjoyed immense success, for the sheer variety of sports events allows for the myriad forms of competition that differently-abled people require (2009). Rather than a one-size-fits-all approach (as in, who can swim the fastest?), the Paralympics philosophy is to offer greater accommodation, such as sitting volleyball, much like today's special education accommodations in school help students who need these special services.

Even given the track record of the Paralympics, would most of us still cheer for that rare athlete who wishes to transcend the odds just to compete? Isn't this the essence of the American sports movie genre: *Rocky, Rudy, Coach Carter, Cinderella Man, The Express*—all of which look at the value of overcoming great odds just to compete and gain recognition. Yet none of the films glamorized by Hollywood featured an athlete with a fake limb. Yet again, the only actor who wore a prosthetic ever to receive an Academic Award played a man returning from war. Perhaps there is a larger playing field that matters more in the long run, one that will help frame the discussion further.

Answer the questions below in your notebook:

1. What similarities do you notice in these responses?

2. What differences do you notice in these responses?

3. Does one approach—argumentative or explanatory—seem to work better for this conversation?

4. How does either approach allow for sources to speak to each other? To what extent does either approach permit evaluation?

You will have noticed that each time the writer refers to one of the sources, that source is cited. The citation need not be elaborate. Most English teachers will prefer that you use one of the forms adopted by the Modern Language Association (MLA), as you see here with the author's name included in your own text and the year of publication in parentheses. In other academic departments you may be required to use a different format, such as one approved by the American Psychological Association (APA). In any situation you should use the style your instructions indicate.

 Wrapping Up the Unit The wording of the prompt will indicate to you whether you are expected to offer an argumentative or explanatory response, but in either case you can see how the templates help you to gather, evaluate, and organize the source material you will be considering as you prepare your response. There are other modes of synthesis in researched papers—beyond argumentative and explanatory— but the task of using sources in the service of an original argument will remain identical.

Poetry Analysis

Portal 1

**Finding
the Portal**

Analysis by Purpose/
Theme and Technique

Up until now, we have focused on portals that dealt with writing—rhetorical analysis, argument, and synthesis. In the following two units, we will investigate ways to engage in written conversation involving the art of literary analysis. These units will draw upon the writing skills that you have already practiced, even as they will offer extensive instruction in the careful reading of poetry and prose.

Essays that analyze poetry generally focus on the poet's particularly artful use of language. They may celebrate the poet's craft, but they are better—that is, more insightful and ultimately more meaningful—when they show how that craft helps the poet reach the full achievement of the poem. A poem, after all, is not merely a collection of metaphors and rhymes. It is a statement of human experience. We read poetry to understand better what that experience is, and we analyze poetry so that we can arrive at the greatest understanding we are capable of.

By far the most common approach towards reading and analyzing poetry involves an equal measure of **theme** and **technique**. Given the highly specialized nature of poetic language, the poem's technique often suggests themes or ideas that more explicit language would struggle to achieve. Conversely, a poem's theme may be so elegant or sophisticated that the writer may need the special language of poetry to present this theme fully.

**The Reading
Experience**

Reading poetry, however, presents different challenges from reading prose—either fiction or nonfiction—as readers view the literature through several lenses. On one level, you read for more comprehensive meaning, but on another level, you allow your comprehension to be influenced by the style and structure of the language. Poetry often needs multiple readings for clear analysis.

To get started, let's look at the opening of a well-known poem, "Richard Cory," by Edwin Arlington Robinson. Your prompt has asked you to explain how the poem's imagery and tone contribute to its overall meaning. Your thoughts might resemble these:

The first stanza of "Richard Cory" by E.A. Robinson reads:

> Whenever Richard Cory went downtown,
>   We people on the pavement looked at him:
> He was a gentleman from sole to crown,
>   Clean favored, and imperially slim.

The actual reading of this poem is easy, given the steady cadence and regular rhyme; the imagery itself presents no real ambiguity. We see the image of a gentleman, fit and trim, bearing a striking pose. The final stanza of the poem reads:

> So on we worked, and waited for the light,
>   And went without the meat, and cursed the bread;
> And Richard Cory, one calm summer night,
>   Went home and put a bullet through his head.

By the last stanza, the imagery and tone have changed, and the fate of Richard Cory compels readers to reconsider—to reread—the earlier parts of the poem to determine the reasons for this fate. One response may focus on the very cadences and rhymes from the first stanza. In other words, the easygoing nature of the writing deceives your perception of him, much in the way that the superficial appearances of Richard Cory deceive the onlookers. Some readers even go so far as revisit the meaning of the name—"rich to the core," so to speak, as if to suggest the hollowness of a man who has devoted all to fortune.

Analysis by purpose/theme and technique, then, looks at the equal measure of form and content.

Thematic Analysis of a Poem
Via Poetic Technique

The following graphic provides an example of how the analysis of technique helps explicate a theme:

Stanza #	Imagery
first	Sole to crown
last	Bullet through his head
Explication of theme	Appearances deceive

Stanza #	Rhyme
first	Downtown and crown—emphasizes urbanity, wealth
last	Bread and head—emphasizes contrast
Explication of theme	What fulfills and what troubles us may not be that far apart.

Stanza #	Symbol
first	Richard Cory—rich to the core, or his 'soul'
last	Light—symbol of hope
Explication of theme	Hope or faith in money is deadly.

It is important to remember, however, that poetic techniques do not work in isolation from each other. A poem may use symbolism and sound devices in the same phrase or word, so your analysis needs to explore the inter-relationship between techniques in the service of supporting meaning.

The Writing Experience

Like written rhetorical analysis, analysis of poetry responds to two main questions: **What is being said?** and **How is it being said?** But unlike rhetorical analysis, the "how" carries greater weight, perhaps no greater in importance than the poem's theme, but greater than the "how" you may write about in rhetorical analysis. Included here may be a poem's **purpose**, and while you may consider purpose to be more a part of a rhetorical task, poems can be rhetorical and thus present a clearer message or purpose.

The keys to writing an effective essay of analysis by purpose or theme and technique are:

- observing techniques that help the poem communicate its meaning;
- explaining the relationship between those technical elements and the overall meaning;
- avoiding summary or paraphrase as a substitute for analysis.

To help you write a literary analysis by purpose/theme and technique, examine the following templates. Think of these templates not only as a road map of what direction to take in your writing, but also as a useful vocabulary for this direction.

Templates for Analysis by Purpose/Theme and Technique

▼ Introducing theme or purpose

These templates provide a statement of the poem's overall meaning.

The theme of the poem is that _____.

By writing _____, the poem's _____ tone communicates the message that____.

The real purpose of the poem is to _____.

Beyond the literal imagery, the poem suggests _____.

▼ Connecting technique to purpose

These templates show the relationship between a technique and the reason the poet used the technique.

The idea of *X* is paralleled by the use of **technique Y**.

The **technique Y** reinforces the idea that _____.

The _____ motif supports the belief that _____.

The repetition of **technique Y** indicates that _____.

▼ Combining techniques

These templates allow for development of more complicated responses to the poem.

Both visual and auditory elements combine to create _____.

Structurally, message *X* is presented through a series of _____.

The theme of _____ is supported not only by the extensive imagery, but also by the connotative diction used to present such imagery.

The poem's meaning and technique work in tandem; one cannot understand the significance of *X* without noting the key relationship between **techniques *Y* and *Z*.**

▼ Monitoring shifts in technique or purpose

These templates are useful when you want to discuss a change in the poet's use of a particular element.

A shift in tone occurs when _____ in order to present this idea:_____.

In order to emphasize the belief that _____, the pace of the poem_____.

By the end of the poem, the imagery becomes, once again, _____.

Breaks in the pattern occur periodically in order to emphasize _____.

▼ Encouraging a linear progression in writing

These templates help you to show the relationship of one part of the poem to another.

If the imagery conveys _____, then the auditory devices also serve to communicate _____.

In addition to the poem's effective use of **technique *Y*,** the poem's overall structure reveals that _____.

The theme of the poem takes on a new meaning halfway through:_____.

The poem develops its thinking that ____ with each new stanza.

A review of the poem's enjambment/organization/structure parallels the ways in which the poem's message evolves.

At first glance, the imagery suggests _____; a symbolic view, however, reveals _____.

Metaphorically, this means _____.

On a symbolic level, the poem asserts _____.

One must also consider the connotation of _____.

Review these templates frequently so that you can utilize their forms and content for future analysis of a poem's technique.

The Conversation Begins

A standard prompt often features these two tasks:

Determine the poet's theme on a given topic and **analyze** the poetic devices he or she uses to communicate that theme.

Notice how each task in the prompt utilizes one of the two questions: What is being said? (determine the poet's theme) and How is it being said? (analyze the poetic devices). Notice how these questions appear again in the prompt below.

Guided Practice

Step 1: *Reading the text*

Read the sample text and prompt.

> Read the following poem entitled "Man Writes Poem" by Jay Leeming. Determine what you perceive to be the writer's tone, and write an essay in which you explain what that tone is and how the various elements of the poem contribute to your perception. If you think the tone changes from one part of the poem to another, explain what causes that shift in your perception.

"MAN WRITES POEM"

This just in a man has begun writing a poem
in a small room in Brooklyn. His curtains
are apparently blowing in the breeze. We go now
to our man Harry on the scene, what's

5   the story down there Harry? "Well Chuck
he has begun the second stanza and seems
to be doing fine, he's using a blue pen, most
poets these days use blue or black ink so blue

is a fine choice. His curtains are indeed blowing

10 in a breeze of some kind and what's more his radiator
is 'whistling' somewhat. No metaphors have been written yet,
but I'm sure he's rummaging around down there

in the tin cans of his soul and will turn up something
for us soon. Hang on—just breaking news here Chuck,
15 there are 'birds singing' outside his window, and a car
with a bad muffler has just gone by. Yes ... definitely

a confirmation on the singing birds." Excuse me Harry
but the poem seems to be taking on a very auditory quality
at this point wouldn't you say? "Yes Chuck, you're right,
20 but after years of experience I would hesitate to predict

exactly where this poem is going to go. Why I remember
being on the scene with Frost in '47, and with Stevens in '53,
and if there's one thing about poems these days it's that
hang on, something's happening here, he's just compared the curtains

25 to his mother, and he's described the radiator as 'Roaring deep
with the red walrus of History.' Now that's a key line,
especially appearing here, somewhat late in the poem,
when all of the similes are about to go home. In fact he seems

a bit knocked out with the effort of writing that line,
30 and who wouldn't be? Looks like ... yes, he's put down his pen
and has gone to brush his teeth. Back to you Chuck." Well
thanks Harry. Wow, the life of the artist. That's it for now,

but we'll keep you informed of more details as they arise.

Jay Leeming

Step 2: *Pre-writing*

Discourse Questions Prior to answering the prompt, record your responses to the following questions:

1. What line(s) present an implicit or explicit statement of the poet's purpose?

2. What does the language present that is visually remarkable?

3. What does the language present that is aurally remarkable?

4. How does the structure of the poem influence its meaning?

5. Where do you see shifts—in tone? in pace? in meaning?

6. How does the poem's persona come across?

Here is a graphic organizer that will help you to gather information from the poem as you prepare your analysis. As you observe various features of the poem in your graphic organizer, see if you can identify templates that would be useful if you were to develop these observations into paragraphs in an essay.

Stanza number	Imagery	Figurative language	Sound devices	Rhythmic devices
1				
2				
3				
4				
5				
6				
7				
8				
9				

Of course, it is likely that you will not have material to place into every space in the chart. Perhaps there is no useful observation to make about a particular technique at all. In this poem, for example, the poet has not used rhyme, and there seems to be no reason to point that out, unless you can make a case for the absence of rhyme as a meaningful element in the overall experience of the poem. Until you know that a particular element is not going to be useful in your analysis, you are better off considering it, and dismissing it only when you are confident your analysis will not make use of it.

You might want to use a graphic organizer like the one above to help you complete other poetic analyses in the future.

Guided Practice

Step 3: *Writing and integrating templates*

Listening In Let's listen to how one voice may use the templates in an analysis by technique.

1st sample response to Jay Leeming prompt

Jay Leeming's ironic view of the artistic process—including the ways in which the public interprets art—presents a somewhat satiric view of the relationship between artist and the public. Adopting the persona of a headlines commentator, "Man Writes Poem" pokes fun at the often arbitrary definitions of what makes great art, partly because of our media-frenzied culture; and yet, Leeming's poem effectively emulates the very techniques of carefully wrought poetry.

The overall structure of the poem reinforces the headline atmosphere of the poem. Each stanza repeats the language of the preceding ones such that the announcer, Harry, actually comments on the behavior of the poet while it is occurring. For example, in the second stanza Harry announces that the poet has "begun the second stanza"; to further the ironic twist, Harry provides mundane imagery, noting—rather absurdly—that "poets these days use blue or black ink." As the poem progresses, this circular structure continues. In the third stanza, Harry notes the outdoor imagery of the blowing breeze and radiator whistling, while in the fourth stanza Harry notes that the poet has moved towards an "auditory quality."

What becomes clearer as the poem progresses is the often elusive nature of poetic inspiration, and again, the poem seems to be turning on itself when Chuck, the anchorman from this fictionalized newscast, invokes both past and present when the poet describes the radiator as "Roaring deep/ with the red walrus of History." Again, acting in parody of its own process, this forced allusion to a ridiculous image—a "red walrus of History," whatever that means—presents a whimsical approach towards the creative process, while at the same time mocking the credence that so much of the public willingly gives to artistic endeavor, independent of the effort or rigor.

When Harry states that "the similes are about to go home" and that the poet is "a bit knocked out with the effort" of writing about the red walrus, the poem reaches its most absurd moment, for it moves from being ironic or humorous, into a slightly more critical approach towards our willingness to publicize ordinary events in the name of a faux art. Even the final line—acting as a type of coda to these steps of the breaking news—suggests that the news itself is more substantive than the artistic content.

Identification of templates

Template to introduce tone

Connection of technique to meaning

Template to encourage linear writing

Combining techniques to inform meaning

Development of shift/linear writing

The enjambment also serves to highlight the distinction between artistic futility and media over-reaction. The reporter Harry notes that "No metaphors have been written yet/ but I'm sure he's rummaging around down there/ in the tin cans of his soul." The irony, of course, is that Harry's language itself metaphorically conveys the emptiness of the writer, as does the mockery of a poet unable to think creatively when Harry notes later on in the poem that "all of the similes are about to go home." Each stanza begins with the completion of an unfinished thought in the previous stanza, reinforcing the random or incoherent nature of artistic endeavor; throughout the poem, these opening lines appear humorous, almost unpoetic in their nature.

Metaphoric interpretation

The imagery itself reinforces this shift from irony to criticism. The predominant imagery at the beginning of the poem—though stereotypic—conveys traditional poetic imagery: birds singing, curtains blowing, a breeze. The imagery becomes two-dimensional, however, as great poets' names are referred to as new events in time—perhaps parodying allusions. And by the end of the poem, the whining radiator complements an exhausted poet whose next major move is to brush his teeth. To a news audience, the statement of "Wow, the life of the artist" might bear irony; to a more detached observer, such a statement communicates clear criticism of a culture driven by instant stardom at the hands of the paparazzi. And the colloquial language matches the imagery: "That's it for now" parallels the hollow quality of the actors, the absence of any auditory significance in the poem, and the frozen sterility of the creative process.

Connecting technique to meaning

Commentary

Notice how in each paragraph of the essay the focus on the analysis is communicated first through one of the templates. The template

> Structurally, message *X* is presented through a series of
> _____.

appears in the first body paragraph as

> The overall structure of the poem reinforces the headline
> atmosphere of the poem.

The template

> A shift in tone occurs when _____ in order to present
> this idea:_____.

is used in the final paragraph, where the writer is most explicitly combining commentary on theme and technique, in this sentence:

> The imagery itself reinforces this shift from irony to criticism.

Nowhere is an observation made about the technique of the poet without an accompanying explanation of how that technique contributes to the overall meaning of the poem or the experience of the reader in reading the poem.

Guided Practice

Step 4: *Application of the templates*

The previous example was one writer's response to the prompt that appeared with the poem. It used some of the templates that appear on pages 104–106, and you had a chance to see how those templates assisted the writer in the task of analyzing the poem. Here is another writer's response to the same prompt and the same poem. See if you can find the templates this writer used, and indicate not only where they are, but also what function they serve in the analysis.

2nd sample response to Jay Leeming prompt

Jay Leeming's "Man Writes Poem" communicates a tone of playfulness, mostly through its syntax and use of stock phrases one might associate with a news broadcast. The character of the speaker, a news commentator named Harry who is reporting the incident to the ostensible anchorman, Chuck, provides much of this playful tone. The poem in fact purports to be a news flash about a topic not normally covered in a regular news program, so the irony of the unexpected subject matter also contributes to the amusing and amused expression of attitude.

The poem's opening tells us immediately that this is going to be an unconventional announcement. The ungrammatical and unpunctuated first line, which becomes a run-on sentence, clues us in to the playful nature of the poem. "This just in" suggests urgency—we have to stop what we're doing so as to give our full attention to this new information. And what is it? A cease-fire in a war-torn zone? A significant new piece of legislation? Some natural cataclysm? The death of a world leader? No. A man has begun to write a poem. Other bits of information presented with equal urgency include the birds singing in line 15, the noisy car in line 16, and the sudden metaphor of mother-like curtains, or a curtain-like mother—we don't know which—in lines 24 and 25. Harry's tendency to treat every detail as newsworthy calls to mind the self-important character of those who deliver the local evening news on our television sets, and here the author uses that tendency to mock Harry and Chuck, and to create the poem's playful tone.

The language of the news broadcast appears conspicuously in Harry's delivery. "Hang on—just breaking news here Chuck" in line 14 sounds like the typical reporter on the street, and "definitely a confirmation," which spans two stanzas between lines 16 and 17, does the same. Chuck interrupts with what sounds like a prepared question, the kind that allows the reporter to sound as though he had prepared extensively for this assignment, and Harry reminds the reader (or the viewer) of his own experience and expertise in the matter of poetry reporting. But even Harry's reminiscing about the old days with the great poets must take a back seat to "hang on, something's happening here" in line 24. The man writing the poem has used a metaphor.

Also contributing to the poem's playful tone is the triviality of what Harry considers significant. We readers learn nothing of what the newly written is poem is about, but we are told the color of ink the poet uses (along with the sage assurance that most poets use blue or black ink), and the obvious generalization that this poem is heavy on auditory imagery. Harry wants his listeners to believe he is knowledgeable about poetry, so he drops the names of Robert Frost and Wallace Stevens (line 22), but he says nothing about them or their work; in fact, just before he makes any remark about them he interrupts himself to report that the current poet has used a couple of metaphors. These unusual comparisons, one of his mother to curtains and the other containing the remarkable expression "the red walrus of History" (line 26), would be interesting to examine—in fact, "the red walrus of History" is a very imaginative expression—but the speaker does not offer any further comment, and without any opportunity to understand it better, we readers are left thinking it sounds somewhat ridiculous. Harry says only, "that's a key line," and acknowledges that after such an exertion the poet must need a rest.

And he does too, so Harry's commentary, and the poem, end.

Wrapping Up the Portal You will probably agree that even though these two writers make somewhat different observations about the poem, both answer the prompt, and both provide valid readings of the poem. We do not present two responses to the prompt to demonstrate that one is right and one is wrong, or even that one is better than the other, but that through careful reading and judicious application of the templates, different writers can produce different successful results.

Analysis by Argument

While the analysis of poetry often follows traditional literary routes—such as determining an overarching theme, assessing a persona, analyzing an attitude or effect—poetry can also operate rhetorically. That is, you can look at how different poetic techniques allow poets to create arguments or make persuasive cases.

Some poems are highly descriptive, and suggest that the poet's chief interest is in sharing that description with the reader. The opening stanza of Keats's "The Eve of St. Agnes," for example, contains such effective imagery of winter that it is widely regarded as one of the chilliest stanzas in all of English poetry. See what you think.

Excerpt from "The Eve of St. Agnes"

1   St. Agnes' Eve—Ah, bitter chill it was!
    The owl, for all his feathers, was a-cold;
    The hare limp'd trembling through the frozen grass,
    And silent was the flock in woolly fold:
5   Numb were the Beadsman's fingers, while he told
    His rosary, and while his frosted breath,
    Like pious incense from a censer old,
    Seem'd taking flight for heaven, without a death,
    Past the sweet Virgin's picture, while his prayer he saith.

John Keats

These lines would provide good material for analysis by technique, with an emphasis on imagery.

But other poems present ideas, and they are less likely to inspire analysis by technique than they are analysis by argument. In these cases the poet seems to want the reader to put him- or herself into a situation, and by creating this vicarious experience for the reader, the poet is actually inviting entry into an argument—not a violent one or a fist fight, but a contemplation of ideas. The poet may advocate one position over another or simply present the ingredients for a good discussion. In either case, **analysis by argument** is a good way to respond to these poems.

Sara Teasdale's "Barter" is a good example of this kind of poem.

"Barter"

Life has loveliness to sell,
All beautiful and splendid things,
Blue waves whitened on a cliff,
Soaring fire that sways and sings,
5   And children's faces looking up
Holding wonder like a cup.

Life has loveliness to sell,
Music like a curve of gold,
Scent of pine trees in the rain,
10   Eyes that love you, arms that hold,
And for your spirit's still delight,
Holy thoughts that star the night.

Spend all you have for loveliness,
Buy it and never count the cost;
15   For one white singing hour of peace
Count many a year of strife well lost,
And for a breath of ecstasy
Give all you have been, or could be.

Sara Teasdale

While highly descriptive, the poem presents an opinion with which the reader might agree or disagree. It seems as though attention to the imagery, as you might have paid in the Keats example, would not be enough. Here we need to evaluate the position the poet is taking. Hence, we find ourselves ready to analyze the argument of the poem.

The Reading Experience

Analysis by argument treats the poem as a logical argument. Unlike rhetorical analysis, where the explicit language directly drives the argument, poetry presents argument *indirectly*, and even though you may determine the various stages of the poem's argument by working your way down the poem, your challenge remains to see how the poem reveals its argument by the end.

Sometimes poems will conclude with an explicit statement of a position, as Sara Teasdale does in "Barter" above, or as Robert Frost writes, asserting quite the opposite attitude toward the individual's response to beauty, at the end of "Stopping by Woods on a Snowy Evening":

But I have promises to keep,

And miles to go before I sleep.

Despite the metaphoric language representing life's journey, the persona of the poem reveals his belief that he cannot stay and watch the beautiful snowfall in the woods. He cannot "give all [he has] been, or could be." He must keep his promises.

The Writing Experience

As in the top-down analysis of traditional rhetoric, when writing an analysis of a poem's argument you work your way down the poem from beginning to end, exploring how the text's message evolves and concludes. But unlike traditional rhetorical analysis—where meaning resides somewhere between the speaker/writer, audience, and subject matter—poetry as argument broadens the discussion into more universal arenas. Rhetorical analysis is timely; analysis of poetry, because of poetry's reliance on figurative language, often invites more abstract, timeless, or universal readings.

Shakespeare's sonnets are among the most rhetorical poems ever written. As you read Shakespeare's sonnet 116, "Let me not to the marriage of true minds," read the accompanying annotation for the analysis of the poem's argument. For the sake of clarity, the sonnet has been divided into four sections: three quatrains and the couplet. Notice the annotations that observe how the poem's argument is evolving.

"Let me not to the marriage of true minds"

Annotation: poetry as argument

Let me not to the marriage of true minds
Admit impediments. Love is not love
Which alters when it alteration finds,
Or bends with the remover to remove:

Initial claim: Nothing can get in the way of 'true love,' not even if a person leaves. True love never alters.

5 O, no! it is an ever-fixed mark,
That looks on tempests and is never shaken;
It is the star to every wandering bark,
Whose worth's unknown, although his height be taken.

The use of natural imagery defines the magnitude of true love; yet, there is a hint of exaggeration, perhaps a possibility of this being too idealistic. How can one measure love's 'height'?

Love's not Time's fool, though rosy lips and cheeks
10 Within his bending sickle's compass come;
Love alters not with his brief hours and weeks,
But bears it out even to the edge of doom.

The argument becomes even more earnest, extending love to the 'edge of doom,' even beyond death.

If this be error and upon me proved,
I never writ, nor no man ever loved.

Is this a challenge to the many who have fallen out of love? Does it cast love as idealistic as art? Interestingly, the poem's beginning and ending are similar; therefore, the entire argument is bookended by ideals.

William Shakespeare

The Petrarchan sonnet can also present a clear argument, as seen in "Ozymandias" by Percy Byssche Shelley. Read the following poem, as well as the accompanying annotation. For clarity's sake, the poem has been divided into two sections: the octave and sestet.

"Ozymandias"

I met a traveler from an antique land
Who said: Two vast and trunkless legs of stone
Stand in the desert. Near them, on the sand,
Half sunk, a shattered visage lies, whose frown,
5   And wrinkled lip, and sneer of cold command,
Tell that its sculptor well those passions read
Which yet survive, stamped on these lifeless things,
The hand that mocked them, and the heart that fed;

And on the pedestal these words appear:
10   "My name is Ozymandias, king of kings:
Look upon my works, ye Mighty, and despair!"
Nothing beside remains. Round the decay
Of that colossal wreck, boundless and bare
The lone and level sands stretch far away.

Percy Byssche Shelley

The preceding examples involve poems that state a claim at the beginning of the poem. Shakespeare's sonnet defends a "marriage of true minds" and redefines our notion of what true love is. Shelley's sonnet begins with a narrative statement, one that figures into the final argument only after one reads the entire poem, as the persona questions the extent to which man-made achievement or recognition can be timeless.

In both examples the claims evolve as the poems progress. By invoking traditional imagery to define true love Shakespeare raises the question of whether his "marriage of true minds" is a statement more about what marriage ought to be, as if to suggest that love extends as much to the mind as it does to the heart. The argument of "Ozymandias" takes on greater irony, given the barren wasteland of the former king.

And both poems conclude with refined versions of their claims. Shakespeare defiantly connects his art to love, suggesting that no one can determine the real boundaries of true love. Shelley's persona concludes with an almost mocking quality, suggesting that the old king's grandeur is as fleeting as the traveler's at the poem's opening.

Whether the poem's argument is stated explicitly or not is secondary to the notion that the poem's *final image* presents an important component in understanding the nature of the argument.

Annotation: poetry as argument

The opening eight lines establish a sense of ruin and decay, and also juxtapose the worlds of politics and art. The irony is that the sculptor's work survives amid the hubristic, arrogant rule of the king. What's also noteworthy is that this is all hearsay, so even the persona plays a role in how the legacy is transmitted over the years.

The irony is presented here, as these hubristic lines accompany a barren wasteland, suggesting the temporary quality of life and how quickly we are forgotten.

If analysis of rhetoric answers these two questions—what is being said, and how is it being said?—analysis of literature answers the same two questions, and adds a third:

What universal concern or idea does this text present?

PORTAL POINTS FOR ANALYSIS OF POETRY BY ARGUMENT:

The keys to writing effective essays of poetry analysis by argument are:

- determine what position the poet is taking on the subject covered in the poem;
- observe the techniques that make the poem work for the reader, and decide how much of your analysis needs to deal with them;
- show how the idea of the poem transcends the timely nature of rhetorical analysis and suggests instead the timelessness or universality of the poetic experience.

To help you write an essay of poetry analysis by argument, examine the following templates. Think of these templates not only as a road map of what direction to take in your writing, but also as a useful vocabulary for this direction.

Templates for Analysis by Argument

▼ Opening the argument
These templates will help you introduce the subject of your argument.

The poem's initial claim is that _____.

At first, the poem appears to state that _____.

The poem's explicit goal is to show that _____.

▼ Developing the argument
These templates will begin a discussion of specific points within your argument.

The message changes when the poem states _____.

As the poem progresses, the message _____ evolves.

A second reading of the image, however, suggests that _____.

The symbolism can be interpreted two ways:_____.

The reason that the tone shifts is that _____.

The message becomes more complex when _____.

▼ Poetic technique in support of argument

These templates will incorporate stylistic analysis into your discussion where appropriate.

The **technique X** emphasizes _____ about the message.

Technique X reinforces the idea that _____.

The poet's use of **technique X** parallels the poem's argument.

▼ Identifying the poem's central argument or purpose

These templates will help to unify your discussion with reference to the main idea of the poem.

By the end of the poem, it is clear that _____.

Despite the suggestion that _____, the poem reveals that _____.

The final lines of the poem communicate _____.

Finally, the poem presents its main message: _____.

Who can argue with the claim that _____?

▼ Extending argument into universality

These templates will help you to express the general applicability of the poem's argument and ideas.

_____ applies to everyone.

_____ remains timeless.

_____ represents human beings' desire/propensity for _____.

Such an image/symbol presents an eternal search for _____.

The allusions are clear:_____.

Review these templates frequently so that you can utilize their forms and content for future analysis of poems as argument.

The Conversation Begins

A standard prompt often features these two tasks:

Determine the poet's position on a given topic and **analyze** the ways he or she presents that view.

Notice how, once again, each task in the prompt utilizes one of the two questions: What is being said? (determine the poet's position), and How is it being said? (analyze the ways he or she presents that view). Notice how these questions appear again in the prompt below.

Guided Practice

Step 1: *Reading the text*

The following poem allows for some variation in interpretation, and its final lines might be taken as an expression of either ridicule of the subject or sympathy for it. It is, then, a good stimulus for analysis by argument, since whichever interpretation you lean toward, whether one of these two or yet another, you would need to defend that reading. Read this poem and the prompt that accompanies it. Then, before you read the sample essay that follows, which is one voice's expression of a way to understand the meaning of the poem, think about how the poem speaks to you and what you would say in response.

As you read the sample, try to see how the writer made use of the templates you saw on pages 117 and 118.

It is commonly accepted that the following poem by Stephen Crane—entitled "The Trees in the Garden"—is meant to be read allegorically. That is, characters and objects in the poem function on more than one level simultaneously. A reader's interpretation of the poem will depend on how he or she understands the different possibilities that these characters and objects present.

Read the poem carefully, noting the literal language narrating the events and considering the interpretive possibilities this language presents. Then decide what interpretive possibilities you see in the poem's final three lines (what the tutor says), and determine how those interpretations can affect your sense of the poem's meaning. Write an essay in which you explain how the reader's understanding of the final lines' meaning affects the meaning of the rest of the poem. Avoid merely paraphrasing the poem.

"The Trees in the Garden"

The trees in the garden rained flowers.
Children ran there joyously.
They gathered the flowers
Each to himself.
Now there were some
Who gathered great heaps—
Having opportunity and skill—
Until, behold, only chance blossoms
Remained for the feeble.
Then a little spindling tutor
Ran importantly to the father, crying:
"Pray, come hither!
See this unjust thing in your garden!"
But when the father had surveyed,
He admonished the tutor:
"Not so, small sage!
This thing is just.
For, look you,
Are not they who possess the flowers
Stronger, bolder, shrewder
Than they who have none?
Why should the strong—
The beautiful strong—
Why should they not have the flowers?"
Upon reflection, the tutor bowed to the ground,
"My lord," he said,
"The stars are displaced
By this towering wisdom.

Stephen Crane

Guided Practice

Step 2: *Pre-writing*

Discourse Questions Prior to answering the prompt, record your responses to the following questions:

1. What is the poem's initial claim?

2. In what ways does the poem's claim evolve as you work your way towards the end of the poem?

3. Where do you see remarkable aspects of language that affect the poem's message?

4. Where do you see shifts—in tone? in purpose? in message?

5. To what extent does the persona of the poem influence the message?

6. In what way(s) does the poem's structure help affect the message?

You might want to organize your thinking in a chart like this one:

Line or stanza	claim	what supports your position?	what challenges your position?	how does the poem's language contribute to your analysis?
1				
2				
3				
4				
5				
6				
7				
8				
9				

Guided Practice

Step 3: *Writing and integrating templates*

Listening In Let's listen to how one voice may use the templates in an analysis by argument.

Sample response to Stephen Crane prompt

Identification of templates

The relationship between knowledge and power changes, depending upon how those who hold power view knowledge. In Stephen Crane's poem "The trees in the garden," the poem ends with a deceptive concession to the notion that might equals right, and that some people—by virtue of acquired or inherited ability—will emerge ahead. A second reading of the final three lines, however, suggests the poem's deeper irony, almost a lamentation, that man-made power sees itself as greater than the stars themselves.

The opening claim

This template presents a more complex feature of the claim.

The opening imagery of the poem presents the age-old conflict of the strong versus the weak. A bucolic setting—with Eden-like properties and innocent children running to gather flowers—conveys the image that "only chance blossoms/Remained for the feeble." The symbolism suggests that those who are weak—in spirit or in body—face random fruits, and that nature herself ordains it so. Crane's hyphens highlight those features attributed to issues of equality—opportunity and skill—and they represent privilege of upbringing or extensive training, neither of which is necessarily innate.

Allusion presents universality and timelessness

Analysis of technique furthers argument

Crane suggests that such inequality can be rectified by those with knowledge, despite the rather critical language associated with the tutor, described as a "little spindling" fellow, "crying," as if he were

Argument develops

one of the children, and finding no better word than "thing" to analyze the disparate gains among the children. Not surprisingly, the father chides the tutor, as if the tutor, this "small sage," were one of the children, and the father speaks in a condescending manner. Invoking an almost Social Darwinist approach, he defends the disparity, and the language of his words parallels the highlights of the first half of the poem, for the "beautiful strong," accented by the hyphens, presents an idealized image of what human beings can be.

The tutor's final line—on a first reading—emerges as an acquiescence to the father's dictum, because the tutor is resigned to the knowledge that disparity always exists. Some will always be born with more than others. This disparity knows no bounds. When the tutor states that even the "stars are displaced/By this towering wisdom," he acknowledges that the heavens themselves must obey the laws of mankind, no matter how brutal they may be.

A more explicit statement of the claim

Commentary

You may remember that in Unit 2, where you learned about writing argument, you frequently encountered the phrase "agree with, disagree with, or qualify" a position taken by the writer whose work served as the stimulus for your response to the given prompt. Notice here how this essay takes the same basic approach. The tutor's final words, to which the prompt directs your attention, are

> "My lord," he said,
> "The stars are displaced
> By this towering wisdom."

The essay seeks to align itself with an ironic reading of this remark, but not until it has considered the possibility that the poet may want the tutor to be taken at face value. As in the classic argument, there is the presentation of the claim, a consideration of an alternate interpretation, and then an explanation of the reading the writer wants to support.

Certain modifications of the templates help this writer to achieve this result.

> The message changes when the poem states _____

appears as

> A second reading of the final three lines, however, suggests the poem's deeper irony…

The template

> The poem's explicit goal is to show that _____

is communicated in this sentence:

> When the tutor states that even the "stars are displaced/
> By this towering wisdom," he acknowledges that the
> heavens themselves must obey the laws of mankind, no
> matter how brutal they may be.

This sentence could have read "The poem's explicit goal is to show that the tutor acknowledges that the heavens themselves must obey the laws of mankind, no matter how brutal they may be," but it is improved and made more useful to the argument by integrating important language from the poem. It is sentences like these—and the skill behind their construction—that keep the writing from developing into a formulaic and mechanical expression.

Guided Practice

Step 4: *Application of templates*

You Try It Read the remainder of the analysis of the response to the Crane poem. Identify and analyze the templates used. To assist you, the templates used have been highlighted.

Remainder of sample response to Stephen Crane prompt

Identification and Analysis of Templates

A second reading, however, presents the irony of the tutor's comments, for he suggests that the father's hubris knows no boundaries, not even among the heavens, so how could anyone rightfully expect his children to behave differently? That the speaker of these words is the tutor—presented as the most "feeble" of all the poem's people—also represents the diminished role of knowledge in how matters of equality present themselves. Such "towering wisdom" will only breed greater inequality, and such a mindset dangerously forecasts ethnic cleansing of future eras.

The second reading also recasts our interpretation of the earlier images. The once bucolic setting, which focused more on the action of the children now presents a stark contrast between the "great heaps" and "chance blossoms," or the march towards quantifiable achievement. The "feeble" aspects of the children contrast with the "beautiful strong" description from the father; even the lack of punctuation in his phrase suggests something deeper than condescension, an almost frightening image of an Aryan race who, by virtue of their attractiveness, enjoy a Samson-like strength. When the tutor states that the "stars are displaced," he alludes to a Babel-like approach towards living—an eternal quest for achievement, the next wonder of the modern world.

All children must lose their innocence and leave that archetypal garden of Eden at some point in their lives. How they extend their knowledge and contribution to the "unjust things" of their world, however, will have everything to do with what future gardens are presented for their children. The two readings of the final three lines convey a distinct sadness, though for differing reasons. The first sadness laments the sad reality of the modern world; the second advocates the pursuit of change, with an "admonition" more for those who fail to ensure the responsible use of power.

Wrapping Up the Portal Those poems that lay arguments before their readers often benefit from an approach such as this kind of analysis. Analyzing poetry as an argument expands your scope of skills—and portals—with which to determine a poem's meaning.

Comparison or Contrast of Poetry

Sometimes, in order to grasp the large sweep of our literary tradition, it is necessary to consider more than one poem simultaneously. If you want to understand the Renaissance, for example, reading one sonnet will not be adequate. Even reading several poems by the same author gives a very limited view. If you want to understand how attitudes changed from the Romantic to the Victorian eras, it will not do to read poetry of only one of those periods. To see similarities and differences, we must take in several examples and make our judgments accordingly. **Comparison**, which shows us the similarities between things, and **contrast**, which focuses on the differences, is possible only when there are sufficient items under consideration.

One way to consider the value of comparing or contrasting poetry is to think of old songs or movies that have been remade into newer versions. Why do artists do this? Certainly not just to emulate their predecessors, but also to see the material through a creative lens representative of a new era or a new way of thinking. Another way to look at this is to think of artists who have worked with similar sounds or pictures, and to consider the ways in which the content differs in the two presentations. Both Claude Monet and Georgia O'Keeffe painted flowers, yet each has distinctive styles and purposes. Melissa Etheridge recently performed her version of "Born to Run" on national television in homage to Bruce Springsteen, yet the twenty-year separation between these two songs has allowed not just for a new sound, but also for a new audience. Do the songs of *Jersey Boys*, a show based on popular music of the 1960s, mean the same to the baby boomers who hear it again in the first and second decades of the twenty-first century as it did when they were young, and does it speak the same messages to young audiences today who sit beside by those boomers in the theatres?

Unlike other aspects of analysis—where your interpretation drives much of the essay, and where your interpretation may differ from your neighbor's—the essay of comparison or contrast provides clearer *objectivity* in terms of how two texts speak to each other. In this regard, the comparison or contrast templates begin to resemble those of the synthesis chapter, insofar as you explore how these two perspectives "speak" to each other on a given topic.

And given the immensely wide range of poetic technique and expression available to writers, not to mention the genre of poetry itself as one that has evolved more dramatically over time than other genres, the comparison or contrast task provides a rich and important study in the relationship of form and function.

Even though you see the conjunction "or" in the heading of this portal, often your responsibility is to explore both similarities and differences. "Or" suggests that your task is one or the other, when in reality, texts that speak to each other will almost always have some features in common. In effect, the comparison or contrast portal asks you to consider four distinct areas:

POEM 1		POEM 2
Textual message	⟷	Textual message
Poetic technique	⟷	Poetic technique

Consider too the various permutations possible in these four areas. You may, for instance, consider similarities in messages but differences in technique; conversely, you may see similarities in technique but differences in messages.

For example, note the following two poems that promote the spirit of individuality. The first, by Emily Dickinson, is called "The soul selects her own society—".

"The soul selects her own society—"

The Soul selects her own Society—
Then—shuts the Door—
To her divine Majority—
Present no more—

5   Unmoved—she notes the Chariots—pausing—
At her low Gate—
Unmoved—an Emperor be kneeling—
Upon her mat.

10   I've known her—from an ample nation—
Choose One—
Then—close the Valves of her attention—
Like Stone—

Emily Dickenson

The second poem, by Stephen Crane, is "A man said to the universe":

"A man said to the universe"

A man said to the universe:
"Sir, I exist!"
"However," replied the universe,
"The fact has not created in me
A sense of obligation."

Stephen Crane

Consider the four distinct areas as you organize your response:

Dickinson's message	Crane's message	Similarities	Differences
The persona—at risk to her own security— rejects those aspects of power to preserve her autonomy.	The persona appeals for recognition, yet the quest leaves him empty.	Both seek individuality in the face of conformity. Both present a stone-like presence.	Dickinson's persona understands the sacrifice while she makes it; Crane's does not.

Dickinson's technique	Crane's technique	Similarities-effects	Differences-effects
Rhyme scheme, emphasizing words such as society and majority	Free verse		With the rhyme scheme, there is greater emphasis on place and purpose, such as 'attention' and 'nation.' Free verse presents greater randomness.
Imagery *Emperor*	Imagery *The Universe*	Grandeur against the individual	

One additional point worth making is that the best essays are those that reveal the truths that lie beneath the surface. The reason why poems —or any texts— are juxtaposed is that they present multiple perspectives on the same subject, particularly subjects that have complex or controversial aspects. Much in the way that you enter into a conversation within a certain community of writers, so too do poets or authors of fiction enter into an artistic conversation of sorts, as they present unique portraits—both in content and style—on topics that matter. By comparing and contrasting, you acknowledge multiple ways in which a particular theme is treated, and in so doing, you take an important step into a conversation with two authors simultaneously.

To help you write an analysis using comparison and contrast, examine the following templates. Think of these templates not only as a road map of what direction to take in your writing, but also as useful vocabulary for this direction.

Templates for Analysis by Comparison and Contrast

▼ Introducing how two texts 'speak' to each other or compare/contrast

These templates help you get started in your handling of the two works together.

Both **poet X** and **poet Y** present _____ about _____.

While the message of *X* is _____, the message of *Y* is _____.

The topic of _____ carries great significance for many; two writers who have expressed differing approaches towards this are *X* and *Y*.

▼ Comparison of content

These templates focus on how the poems' messages are similar.

Similar to *X*, *Y* believes _____.

Like *X*, *Y* states _____.

Both poems communicate the idea that _____.

These poems agree that _____.

Both poems conclude with the same message:_____.

▼ Comparison of technique
These templates highlight ways in which the poetic elements are similar.

Both poems' imagery/allusions/symbols/etc. communicate the idea that _____.

Either poet makes extensive use of **poetic technique X** to communicate her or his idea that _____.

Both writers make similar transitions or shifts in terms of _____.

Like poet **X**, poet **Y** explores the way that [poetic technique] communicates his message.

Both poems rely upon a similar structure to present their message.

▼ Contrast of content
These templates allow for a presentation of differences in the two poems' messages.

While poet **X** presents _____, poet **Y** believes _____.

Unlike the message of poem **X**, which states _____, poem **Y** believes otherwise:_____.

Though both poems believe _____, they differ when it comes to _____.

Yes, both poems do address _____, but there are clear differences, especially when it comes to_____.

▼ Contrast of technique
These templates focus on how the poetic elements differ.

Where poem **X** relies heavily on light imagery, poem **Y** relies more on darkness.

Even the auditory aspects of the poem present differences in meaning.

The structural differences between the poem also reveal their differing approaches.

Though the diction may be similar, the connotations and symbols differ.

The comparisons/contrasts provide a useful perspective on _____.

Numerous versions of this story have presented themselves throughout the ages.

Revisiting this topic through the eyes of _____ allows readers to consider . . . .

At issue is more than just how these poets approach _____, but what their messages mean about _____.

▼ **Repetition or Parallelism to emphasize comparison/contrast**
These templates give a balanced structure to your discussion.

For comparison
Both poems communicate _____. Both state _____. Both believe _____. And both convince readers that _____.

For contrast
Poem *X* states ____; poem *Y* states _____; and while *X* notes ____, *Y* offers ____. Even when *X* identifies _____, *Y* offers _____. In short…

Review these templates frequently so that you can utilize their forms and content for future analysis of poems by compare and contrast.

The Conversation Begins

A standard prompt often features these two tasks:

Compare and/or contrast the ways in which two poets present their views on a similar topic, and **explain** the techniques that both poets use to communicate their views.

While this prompt contains some variations to the tasks that appeared in the first two portals, their intent is basically the same. The first instructs you to compare and contrast what is being said, and the second instructs you to analyze how that basic message is communicated. The following prompt presents a further variation in that it asks you to note specific techniques (diction and imagery) in your reading, and then, in your essay, use that information to discuss how the poems compare and contrast in terms of their basic message about World War I.

Step 1: *Reading the text*

> Prominent World War I poets Rupert Brooke and Siegfried Sassoon wrote the following two poems. Read each poem carefully, noting how **each** sonnet makes use of specific diction and imagery. Then, in a well-written essay, compare and/or contrast the two poems' views on World War I.

"The Soldier"

If I should die, think only this of me:
That there's some corner of a foreign field
That is for ever England. There shall be
In that rich earth a richer dust conceal'd;

5 A dust whom England bore, shaped, made aware,
Gave, once, her flowers to love, her ways to roam,
A body of England's, breathing English air.
Wash'd by the rivers, blest by suns of home.
And think, this heart, all evil shed away,

10 A pulse in the eternal mind, no less
Gives somewhere back the thoughts by England given;
Her sights and sounds; dreams happy as her day;
And laughter, learnt of friends; and gentleness,
In hearts at peace, under an English heaven.

Rupert Brooke (1887–1915)

"Trench Duty"

Shaken from sleep, and numbed and scarce awake,
Out in the trench with three hours' watch to take,
I blunder through the splashing mirk; and then
Hear the gruff muttering voices of the men

5 Crouching in cabins candle-chinked with light.
Hark! There's the big bombardment on our right
Rumbling and bumping; and the dark's a glare
Of flickering horror in the sectors where
We raid the Boche; men waiting, stiff and chilled,

10 Or crawling on their bellies through the wire.
'What? Stretcher-bearers wanted? Some one killed?'
Five minutes ago I heard a sniper fire:
Why did he do it? ... Starlight overhead—
Blank stars. I'm wide-awake; and some chap's dead.

Siegfried Sassoon (1886–1967)

Step 2: *Pre-writing*

Discourse Questions Prior to answering the prompt, record your responses to the following questions:

    1. How do the two poems present similar messages?

    2. To what extent do the messages of each text differ?

    3. What are the similarities and differences of poetic technique?

    4. In what way(s) does the persona of each text differ?

    5. In what way(s) does the comparison/contrast illuminate a larger issue?

In your notebook, record your answers in the graphic organizer below.

Comparing these two poems: Brooke, "The Soldier" and Sassoon, "Trench Duty"

	similarities	differences
Technique 1		
Technique 2		
Technique 3		
Message 1		
Message 2		

Guided Practice

Step 3: *Writing and integrating templates*

Read the following sample response. Notice that some of the templates are not identified. Using the list on pages 128–130, see if you can identify the templates used in the sample essay.

 Listening In Let's listen to how one writer compared and contrasted these two poems, using selected templates.

Sample response to Rupert Brooke and Siegfried Sassoon prompt

In the service of one's country during war, one fundamental question all soldiers confront is loyalty—loyalty to one's self, and loyalty to the greater cause of country. In a world where questions about the extent to which service beyond something greater than ourselves has—in its most damaging form—individuals isolated from each other, one also questions whether duty to one's country means the ultimate sacrifice of life. Rupert Brooke and Siegfried Sassoon represent these disparate views towards sacrifice and commitment in the service of England during World War I.

Brooke's "The Soldier" epitomizes the value of service to one's country. The message of his poem is that country comes before the individual. Replete with imagery associated with the English terrain, his ashes would be buried at home—"A body of England's, breathing English air" (line 7). Such imagery actually joins the soldier's physical being with the English countryside; indeed, the persona's opening lines begin with his prediction of death, but that he wants his lasting memory to be some part of a 'foreign field/That is forever England" (lines 3–4). It is as if the soldier's sacrifice extends parts of the British empire into the new land.

The soldier's death takes on a religious aura as the imagery moves to a type of resurrection. The persona identifies "A pulse in the eternal mind" (line 10); his heart continues to beat for something grander, something that "gives somewhere back the thoughts by England given." The repetition of "gives" and "given" (line 11) provides a clear collaboration between soldier and country, from physical to ethereal. The final images of the poem produce a nostalgic effect, as the "sights and sounds" (line 12) illuminate the camaraderie among patriots and friends, all this occurring "under an English heaven" (line 14). That the poem moves from the soldier's death to images of vitality and heaven conveys an inspirational quality, perhaps idyllic, but one worthy of pursuit in a greater cause.

By contrast, Sassoon's "Trench Duty" virtually ignores any thought of God or country, for his poem illuminates the deafening, deadly, existential aspects of going to war. While Brooke's opening image is of a

Identification of templates

Statement of comparison/contrast

[highlighted text reveals parallelism to illustrate comparison/contrast]

dead soldier ready to be resurrected, Sassoon's moves in the opposite direction, presenting a soldier paradoxically "shaken from sleep" but also "numbed" (line 1) by the ongoing percussion of bombardment. Where Brooke identifies laughter and fellowship, Sassoon presents "gruff muttering voices of the men" (line 4). And where Brooke's persona's depiction of England takes on a lyrical, bucolic quality—"a rich earth," "flowers to love," "blest by the suns of home"—Sassoon's cacophonous diction belies a scene in constant turmoil: "crouching in cabins candle-chinked with light" (line 5). Brooke considers light imagery; Sassoon's persona is mired in dark.

Sassoon's poem, rather than pointing to resurrection, identifies the futility of such a sacrifice, for the imagery goes from bad to worse. As the persona describes the raid on the "Boche," what flickers is "horror," rather than light or hope; rather than a mossy field, Sassoon describes both men and barbed wire as "stiff and chilled" (line 9). The successive rhetorical questions about death present an almost whimsical attitude towards death. Perhaps the darkest question is: "Why did he do it?" The pronoun applies equally to the enemy, but also to the soldier who gave his life unwillingly. The "starlight overhead" (line 13) is no heavenly force looking out for Brooke's soldier; rather, these stars are "blank," (line 14) expressionless, disdainful of human error. Sassoon's solider is awake, awaiting death, unaware of what his role is in the grander scheme.

Despite their clear difference in attitude, both poems present variations on the sonnet structure. While both are fourteen lines in length, Brooke's follows a more traditional Elizabethan format, with conventional rhyme scheme and rhythm. Sassoon also presents a clear rhyme scheme and meter, though with variations to the Elizabeth format or iambic pentameter. By acknowledging the sonnet structure, both poets present an awareness—in style—of past conventions, similar to the ways in which thoughts about service or war would be grounded in traditional beliefs. Sassoon's more modern, altered format suggests a more contemporary attitude towards war, one willing to challenge existing conventions.

That Sassoon's poem presents a more despairing, cynical view towards war may represent more contemporary thinking, but given the questions that these two poems present about service to a greater cause, newer may not necessarily be better.

Contrast in technique

Contrast in technique

What the comparisons reveal

What the comparisons reveal

What the comparisons reveal

| Copyright Peoples Education. Photocopying not permitted.

Commentary

This pair of sobering poems would appear to focus on similarities. Two young men, both English soldiers during World War I, write of their experiences in a war that turned out to be more horrible than anyone had expected it to be. We are prepared, when we read the remarkable collection of poetry written by soldiers who fought in the war, to encounter repeated expressions of horror, dismay, pain, despair, and a host of other negative responses to their experiences. So when we are given poems by two of these writers, it is better to focus our attention on how they are different. And that is what this essay does.

In order to show the contrast between the two poems' content, the writer uses this template:

> Unlike the message of poem *X*, which states _____, poem *Y* believes otherwise:_____.

> By contrast, Sassoon's "Trench Duty" virtually ignores any thought of God or country, for his poem illuminates the deafening, deadly, existential aspects of going to war.

The first portion of the template is unnecessary here because the transition it contains is provided in the essay by other means, most significantly structural ones. The second part, which begins "poem *Y* believes otherwise," is made concrete by the specific completion of the statement, how Sassoon's poem ignores the very items Brooke's poem focuses on.

The essay ends with a statement born of the template

> Revisiting this topic through the eyes of _____ allows readers to consider . . . .

The actual sentence that ends the essay is

> That Sassoon's poem presents a more despairing, cynical view towards war may represent more contemporary thinking, but given the questions that these two poems present about service to a greater cause, newer may not necessarily be better.

The author might have written, "Revisiting this topic through the eyes of Sassoon allows readers to consider that newer ideas may not necessarily be better ideas," but the sentence as written embraces the ideas that have run through the entire essay, and relies on the spirit of the template if not the actual wording. As you gain practice in using the templates, your sentences will do the same.

Step 4: *Application of templates*

You Try It Return to the sample response on the World War I poets. Identify the templates used in the middle of the essay. In your notebook, analyze the ways that these four templates further the comparison/contrast of these two poems:

	Template used	Analysis of effect of template
1		
2		
3		
4		

Wrapping Up the Unit Essays of comparison and contrast are very common in many educational situations. Your English teachers will probably assign them in a number of settings, but you are just as likely to need the skills highlighted here in your history classes, your science classes, and several other fields of study. The templates you see in this chapter are also useful when the task is to compare and contrast prose passages, as you will see in the next unit.

Prose Analysis

Portal 1

Finding the Portal

Analysis of Persona

Prose analysis recalls some of your most familiar experiences with reading and writing analytically, especially given that prose analysis is usually based upon works of fiction. One of the earliest tasks you learned as a reader was to determine an author's theme, but as you know from your other analytical experiences, often how the author makes the statement is as important as the statement itself.

The major difference between analyzing prose and analyzing rhetoric is that prose, like poetry, offers universalities, while rhetoric tends to be more topical. But unlike poetry, where form or style carries equal (or more) weight than content, prose analysis presents a middle ground between the worlds of poetry and rhetoric, for though the content is fiction, the messages are truthful.

So, to enter a conversation about the meaning or effect of a work of prose, which in some settings you will do with regard to an excerpt rather than to an entire work, one good place to begin is with the **persona**, or the character of the voice behind the narration. The persona is not the author, even in an autobiography, for the writer of an autobiography must present him- or herself through description and narration, and it is the manner of that presentation that allows the reader to make judgments about that speaker's personality. Auto-biographers, given their subject matter, cannot be entirely objective, and their choices of personae need to be examined and analyzed if we are to understand their works fully. Benjamin Franklin, for example, creates a very entertaining persona in his life story. It is doubtful that another writer telling the story of Franklin's life would speak in the same voice.

The Reading Experience

The **analysis of persona**, or the voice of the speaker, then, answers the question about why writers might employ a fictitious mode rather than a factual one. By removing him- or herself from the actual narrative and instead creating an alternate voice—not to mention fictionalizing names, events, or settings—the persona provides a particular quality that gives significance to the overall narrative, such as the reliability of Nick Carraway in *The Great Gatsby*. One reason Jonathan Swift creates a persona to introduce "A Modest Proposal" is to establish a position somewhere between the writer and the audience, a middle ground that rarely exists in the immediacy of rhetorical analysis. And postmodern writers have developed the art of creating various personae in texts that feature multiple narrators: *As I Lay Dying* by William Faulkner, *Wide Sargasso Sea* by Jean Rhys, and *Mama Day* by Gloria Naylor, to name just a few.

A persona, of course, appears in all forms of writing; even research historians adopt personae through which they present their information. A poem's speaker is always called the persona, for it is the deliberate voice created by the writer. In fact, you are likely to find the term "speaker" used as a synonym for "persona" in poetry, prose, and non-fiction. Thus, when you hear the phrase, "consider the messenger," you should think of the persona as a key instrument in unlocking the meaning of the prose.

When you write, whether it is an analysis of someone else's prose or the creation of your own, you must always be aware of the voice that speaks from the page. You have seen how important the element of tone is in communicating ideas. There is no shortage of examples of cases in which a writer failed to win an audience's trust because the writing communicated an attitude the audience found objectionable, even when the content of the piece was quite acceptable. In most fictional settings we must evaluate the character of the speaker as part of our overall reading experience. In *The Scarlet Letter*, for example, it becomes clear very quickly that the narrator admires, perhaps even loves, Hester Prynne, and that his attitude toward her is at odds with the attitudes of the women gathered around the scaffold in the scene of Hester's first appearance. The novel would be very different if Dimmesdale were telling the story, or if Chillingworth were. Likewise, as you write an analysis of the novel, your own personality, beliefs, biases, and experiences become part of your writing voice, and the degree to which you can shape and use your own persona will certainly influence the final expression of your ideas. Awareness of persona is a crucial matter for both reader and writer.

PORTAL POINTS FOR ANALYSIS OF PERSONA:

When writing essays that analyze a passage's persona, key points to consider are:

- what can we learn about the personality behind the voice telling the story;
- is there one persona in the passage or has the author chosen to have multiple speakers;
- how might the effect of the passage be changed if the presentation had been through someone else's eyes.

To help you write an essay analyzing a persona, examine the following templates. Think of these templates not only as a road map of what direction to take in your writing, but also as a useful vocabulary for this direction.

Templates for Analysis of Persona

Connecting persona to purpose
These templates help you explain why the author chose the particular persona.

Who is presenting **message X** is as important as the way it's being heard.

The narrator, or persona, cannot be an impartial observer.

We come to a clearer understanding about **message X** when we experience **Y** through the eyes and ears of the persona.

Presenting persona as part of a larger context.
These templates help you relate the choice of persona to other elements of the text.

Our interpretation of _____ rests largely within the context of the persona's interpretation.

While the characters may claim _____, the persona's interpretation suggests _____.

The reason the author creates the persona is to present his larger statement, which is:_____.

Persona (or audience) development
These templates help you characterize the persona.

The narrator's language/diction portray him as _____.

The actions of the narrator present a persona capable of _____.

The persona's attitude towards the topic is _____.

The persona's stance towards her audience is _____.

The **techniques X and Y** associated with the characters apply equally to the persona.

Persona as a conduit to evaluation of theme or purpose
These templates relate the persona to the meaning of the work as a whole.

Because the persona herself reveals _____, it is reasonable to conclude that _____.

The persona reveals what no one can articulate: that _____. And the reasons for this are clear:_____.

That the speaker responds in *X* manner means that the following interpretation applies:

At stake is the credibility of the claim that _____.

The truth is evasive, because _____.

Persona and literary technique
These templates connect the persona to other characters in the work.

The speaker's language reveals that _____.

The persona differs from the other characters this way:_____.

The persona complements the characters by illuminating these blind spots:_____.

▼ **Persona's development through audience**
These templates relate the persona to the reader.

The persona represents an objective observer, for he sees that _____.

The _____ nature of the persona influences the story's progress in this way:

The absence of the persona would raise serious questions about _____.

Review these templates frequently, so that you can utilize their forms and content for future analyses of persona.

The Conversation Begins

A standard prompt for a question that encourages an analysis of persona reads as follows:

Analyze the way an author's views on a topic are presented through her or his development of the persona.

Note that the above prompt features **two distinct tasks:**

1. Understanding the way that the author develops the persona, and

2. Understanding the relationship between the persona and the given topic.

Analyzing the persona resembles a top-down approach, whereby you monitor not just the events of the narrative, but also the ways in which the speaker presents him- or herself to you. In some ways, analyzing the persona comes closest to analyzing a real audience's role. To help you compose a successful essay that analyzes the persona, complete the following steps.

Step 1: *Reading the prompt*

Read the following prompt. Note the task as it is presented. You will have to determine something about the persona of the speaker as a representative of the author.

> The following passage comes from the first voyage of Jonathan Swift's *Gulliver's Travels*. Lemuel Gulliver, the speaker, has arrived in the land of Lilliput, where people, animals, and plants are one-twelfth the size of their counterparts in his native England. He becomes a celebrity and an attraction in his new community, and is given a home at the King's court. In this scene the King's Secretary of Private Affairs is explaining some matters of foreign policy to Gulliver.
>
> Read the passage carefully, considering the human behaviors the Secretary describes. Then write an essay in which you analyze the role of the persona in communicating the author's views. Do not substitute summary for analysis.

Step 2: *Pre-writing*

Discourse Questions The following questions will assist both your reading and writing experience.

1. What is remarkable about the ways in which the persona is presented?

2. Is the persona likeable? Reliable? Explain.

3. How does the persona influence the record of key events or statements?

4. What larger themes, issues, or ideas are at stake that make the persona's role in the matter an important one?

5. In what way(s) does the persona's perspective differ from that of others in the prose?

6. How might your response to the scene change if the persona were absent?

Step 3: *Reading the text*

As you read this sample prompt and prepare to compose your response, pay attention to the accompanying annotations that monitor the role of the persona.

Excerpt from Gulliver's Travels, *book I, chapter 4*

Annotation about the persona

One morning, about a Fortnight after I had obtain'd my Liberty, Keldresal, Principal Secretary (as they style him) of private Affairs, came to my House, attended only by one Servant. He ordered his Coach to wait at a distance, and desired I would give him an Hour's
5 Audience; which I readily consented to, on account of his Quality, and Personal Merits, as well as the many good Offices he had done me during my Sollicitations at Court. I offered to lie down, that he might the more conveniently reach my Ear; but he chose rather to let me hold him in my hand during our Conversation. He began with Compli-
10 ments on my Liberty, said he might pretend to some Merit in it; but, however, added, that if it had not been for the present Situation of things at Court, perhaps I might not have obtained it so soon. For, said he, as flourishing a Condition as we may appear to be in to Foreigners, we labour under two mighty Evils; a violent Faction at home,
15 and the Danger of an Invasion by a most potent Enemy from abroad. As to the first, you are to understand, that for above seventy Moons past, there have been two struggling Parties in this Empire, under the Names of Tramecksan, and Slamecksan, from the high and low Heels on their Shoes, by which they distinguish themselves. It is alledged
20 indeed, that the high Heels are most agreeable to our ancient Constitution: But however this be, his Majesty hath determined to make use of only low Heels in the Administration of the Government, and all Offices in the Gift of the Crown, as you cannot but observe; and particularly, that his Majesty's Imperial Heels are lower at least by a
25 Drurr than any of his Court; (Drurr is a Measure about the fourteenth Part of an Inch.) The Animositys between these two Partys run so high, that they will neither eat nor drink, nor talk with each other. We compute the Tramecksan or High-Heels, to exceed us in number; but the Power is wholly on our side. We apprehend his Imperial High-
30 ness, the Heir to the Crown, to have some Tendency towards the High-Heels; at least, we can plainly discover one of his Heels higher than the other, which gives him a Hobble in his Gait. Now, in the midst of these intestine Disquiets, we are threatned with an Invasion from the Island of Blefuscu, which is the other great Empire of the Universe,
35 almost as large and powerful as this of his Majesty. For as to what

The deadpan quality of this statement suggests the persona may not be altogether serious.

The persona is being lectured to by Keldresal.

The absurdity of the imagery is presented by his condescending tone.

Gulliver's distance from the topic helps convey the fear-mongering mindset of the Lilliputians.

we have heard you affirm, that there are other Kingdoms and States in the World, inhabited by human Creatures as large as yourself, our Philosophers are in much doubt, and would rather conjecture that you dropt from the Moon, or one of the Stars; because it is certain, that an

40 hundred Mortals of your Bulk would, in a short time, destroy all the Fruits and Cattle of his Majesty's Dominions. Besides, our Historys of six thousand Moons make no mention of any other Regions, than the two great Empires of Lilliput and Blefuscu. Which two mighty Powers have, as I was going to tell you, been engaged in a most obstinate War

45 for six and thirty Moons past. It began upon the following Occasion. It is allowed on all hands, that the primitive way of breaking Eggs before we eat them, was upon the larger End: But his present Majesty's Grandfather, while he was a Boy, going to eat an Egg, and breaking it according to the ancient Practice, happened to cut one of his

50 Fingers. Whereupon the Emperor his Father published an Edict, commanding all his Subjects, upon great Penaltys, to break the smaller End of their Eggs. The People so highly resented this Law, that our Historys tell us there have been six Rebellions raised on that account; wherein one Emperor lost his Life, and another his Crown. These civil

55 Commotions were constantly formented by the Monarchs of Blefuscu; and when they were quelled, the Exiles always fled for Refuge to that Empire. It is computed, that eleven thousand Persons have, at several times, suffered Death, rather than submit to break their Eggs at the smaller End. Many hundred large Volumes have been published upon

60 this Controversy: But the Books of the Big-Endians have been long forbidden, and the whole Party rendred incapable by Law of holding Employments. During the Course of these Troubles, the Emperors of Blefuscu did frequently expostulate by their Embassadors, accusing us of making a Schism in Religion, by offending against a fundamental

65 Doctrine of our great Prophet Lustrog, in the fifty-fourth Chapter of the Brundecral, (which is their Alcoran.) This, however, is thought to be a meer Strain upon the Text: For the Words are these; That all true Believers shall break their Eggs at the convenient End: and which is the convenient End, seems, in my humble Opinion, to be left to every

70 Man's Conscience, or at least in the power of the Chief Magistrate to determine. Now the Big-Endian Exiles have found so much Credit in the Emperor of Blefuscu's Court, and so much private Assistance and Encouragement from their Party here at home, that a bloody War hath been carried on between the two Empires for six and thirty Moons

75 with various Success; during which time we have lost forty Capital Ships, and a much greater number of smaller Vessels, together with thirty thousand of our best Seamen and Soldiers; and the Damage received by the Enemy is reckoned to be somewhat greater than Ours. However, they have now equipped a numerous Fleet, and are just pre-

The speaker here exhibits the very same over-reactions to small events that he earlier warns against.

80 paring to make a Descent upon us; and his Imperial Majesty placing
great Confidence in your Valour and Strength, hath commanded Me to
lay this Account of his Affairs before You.

   I desired the Secretary to present my humble Duty to the Emperor,
and to let him know, that I thought it would not become Me, who was a
85 Foreigner, to interfere with Partys; but I was ready, with the hazard of
my Life, to defend his Person and State against all Invaders.

While Gulliver appears obedient, his account of this event suggests his grave doubts.

Jonathan Swift

A simple T-chart will help you gather and arrange information about
the persona:

Analyzing the persona of _____	
Event or description	**What does it tell me about the persona?**

**Guided
Practice**

Step 4: *Speaking first, then listening in*

You Try It Up until now you have entered the conversation by first listening to others. In this chapter, you will have the opportunity to first use the
information culled from these earlier steps to begin writing your response.
To that end, write the first 250 words of your response in your notebook,
and underline those sentences that make active use of the templates. In the
margin on the right, identify the templates that you have used. Your writing
should look something like this graphic organizer.

Original response to Jonathan Swift prompt: first 250 words	Identification of templates used

Listening In Now, listen in to the sample response. Read the sample response and templates used. Observe how your own use of templates compares with those in the sample response.

Sample response to Jonathan Swift prompt

Gulliver's account of how the Lilliputians deal with problems in their society reflects the tendency of people to exaggerate the importance of matters, and in so doing, to go overboard in legislating human behavior. Gulliver's subtle but clear humor presents his (and the readers') quizzical, if not bemused, look at the over-reacting Lilliputians.

The Secretary of Private Affairs—itself a paradoxical position—presents a seemingly threatening scenario, where matters at home and abroad pose equal threats. While the Secretary's tone is urgent and sincere, his diction belies an exaggerated quality, so as to convey Gulliver's implied incredulity at the severity of the problem. That the violent factions are noted as "high and low" heels mocks the usual prejudices that accompany xenophobic societies, and how fitting it is that the label of difference here has to do with the size of one's heel. Even the fictitious names of the factions—*Tramecksan* and *Slamecksan*, as well as the island Blefuscu—bear an outrageous quality and increase the buffoonery of the foreign policy.

How the Secretary's office deals with these problems appears second to how the Secretary manages to find more superficial allies, comrades whose gait or height do not somehow threaten the position of the Secretary, as if to suggest that all subordinates must be perpetually lower than the authority. Gulliver implies as much by initially offering to lie down so as to allow the speaker to reach his Ear, a movement not so much condescending as it is practical. Gulliver ironically notes the "hobble in [one's] gait" that comes from trying to put on airs, or "heirs," in an effort to raise one's self, and so one must sink to the lowest common denominator, lest feathers are ruffled.

Small wonder, then, that the crises that are referred to have less to do with the foreigner (perhaps coined by joining 'fourteenth' and *Drurr*?) and more to do with ruffling the feathers of the home office. Superficially, the Lilliputians are concerned with an invasion from Blefuscu, a neighboring island, and refuse to believe that other mortals outside of Gulliver exist. Their insular, myopic approach to problems prevents them from entertaining a knowledge outside of their own history books; Gulliver wryly notes that "it is certain" that Mortals such as Gulliver would easily destroy all the resources of a kingdom. Swift satirizes the behavior of western greed and consumption, and its emissaries such as Gulliver do pose a threat to the Lilliputians, given the disparity in their sizes. Yet the Lilliputians would rather close their eyes to this potential hegemony, instead preferring to focus on

Identification of templates used

Connecting persona to purpose

Presenting persona as part of a larger context

Persona (or audience) development through action

Persona as a conduit to evaluation of theme or purpose

more minute matters, such as which side of the egg to break first. The absence of logic is also reflected in Gulliver's report, as much of the syntax begins with conjunctions or fragments, as if to suggest an irrationality of thought or an unwillingness to establish clear connections between ideas. The Secretary's speech, riddled with non-sequiturs, reveals as much about his own people as it does about his ability to deal with problems.

Persona and technique

And what is the biggest problem presented? How to break an egg. Parodying the monarchial, dictatorial approach towards the creation of laws—because of something as superficial as a flesh wound—Gulliver notes how this conflict ultimately led to the civil war, and that thousands have willingly suffered death rather than break their eggs at the smaller end. The edicts, however, extend beyond legal principle into the moral, religious grounds, as the treatise against the egg-breakers invokes even more obscure liturgy from the island's religion.

Persona and purpose

It does appear that the Lilliputians wish for a greater sense of their own autonomy, for the commanders of Blefuscu have oppressed them for their unwillingness to engage in such a trivial matter. The formal, militant language of the Secretary's account suggests that such matters are taken seriously by all parties involved, and there is no recourse but to resort to violence to find a solution to such a minor problem. The Lilliputians have little to fall back on in these matters, for neither law nor moral code nor codified practice seems capable of deciphering what the "convenient" end of an egg truly is. In the end, it appears, size does matter, as all the Secretary seems to want is for the giant Gulliver to help win the war against the enemy.

Persona's development through audience

Commentary

The prompt for this essay question asked for the writer to "analyze the role of the persona in communicating the author's views," and to avoid summarizing the plot. The persona here is, as is true in many works of literature, the author's vehicle for disseminating his views, so the question is a natural one. It is important to address both parts of the task—the views of the author and the role of persona in communicating them. An essay that discusses only the author's views will be unsatisfactory.

Several of the templates were useful in helping the writer express the persona's character and his role in this narrative. The template reads:

> While the characters may claim _____, the persona's interpretation suggests _____.

and the actual sentence in the essays becomes:

> While the Secretary's tone is urgent and sincere, his diction belies an exaggerated quality, so as to convey Gulliver's implied incredulity at the severity of the problem.

The writer is using the contrast between the Secretary's tone and Gulliver's reaction to it to suggest a facet of Gulliver's character. This characterization is necessary in order to show Gulliver's (and perhaps then Swift's) position on the problems of Lilliput.

Another template that relates the character of the speaker to the thematic implications of the narrative is:

> The _____ nature of the persona influences the story's progress in this way.

In this analysis the essay writer has composed

> The formal, militant language of the Secretary's account suggests that such matters are taken seriously by all parties involved…

This sentence combines the observation about the language of the Secretary with the judgment of the persona, and ultimately, the intent of the author.

Wrapping Up the Portal One of the biggest dangers in an essay of this type is the tendency to fall into plot summary. You might think you are analyzing the persona when you are actually doing little more than retelling the story. Careful and conscious use of the templates suggested here can help you avoid that pitfall and produce instead an essay that really focuses on the nature of the persona and his or her relationship to the passage's themes.

Finding the Portal

The Reading Experience

The Writing Experience

Analysis of Effect or Technique

Observing specific aspects of prose may also lead to an awareness that an author has used a particular **technique** for a specific **purpose**. For example, you may explore humor as the way Oscar Wilde reflects his views on aristocratic England in *The Importance of Being Earnest*; or setting and mood as the means by which Nathaniel Hawthorne personifies the forest and uses that personification to complement the darker secrets of the human heart; or a remarkable configuration of color imagery, as seen in F. Scott Fitzgerald's opening of chapter two of *The Great Gatsby,* where Nick describes the Valley of Ashes, Wilson's garage, and George Wilson himself in various shades of gray.

When you analyze an author's handling of a certain effect, you are monitoring the recurrence of an element that contributes to the greater whole. If, for example, you explore how the author develops mood, which is to say how the author manipulates the reader's feelings, then you examine the range of elements that help contribute to that mood, elements which may include imagery, dialogue, conflict, and symbolism. Similarly, if you are analyzing an author's use of humor, your reading and writing tasks become an analysis of the ways in which the various aspects of humor—incongruity, juxtaposition, distortion—combine to help produce the desired effect.

Similar to some aspects of rhetorical analysis, particularly in the examination of memoir, the written task becomes less linear—as it would in a top-down analysis—and more an interconnected series of techniques, a type of landscape that is created through your reading.

One of the most attractive risks when writing an **analysis of effect or technique** as has been noted about analysis of persona, is to fall without realizing it into plot summary. While this is a risk in all essays of literary analysis, it seems to be especially problematic when you are writing about an author's literary style. You worry that unless the reader of your essay is familiar with the story, comments about the use of language won't make much sense. While that is true to some degree, it is not true to the degree that you must give a full account of the plot. A good rule to follow is to assume that your audience has some familiarity with your material—not as much as you, of course, because if your reader already had the insight that your essay is going to demonstrate, there wouldn't be much point in your writing that essay for that reader. So imagine an audience who has read the novel or play, perhaps some time ago, and knows the basic content, but needs some gentle reminders of some of the details.

The sample essay on *Gulliver's Travels* that appears earlier in this chapter can illustrate this approach to writing. If you know the novel well, you should have had no difficulty in following the essay and understanding the appropriateness of the comments on it. But if you are not familiar with the novel, did you find that the essay made no sense at all? Was it impossible to understand who the characters were or what the basic situation was? As an unfamiliar reader you might have been puzzled if the essay had said that the Lilliputians were fearful of attack from Blefuscu. If you had never read *Gulliver's Travels* you would of course have no idea who or what Blefuscu is. But if you had read the book and had forgotten, a phrase like "Blefuscu, a neighboring island," tells you all you need to jog your memory and does not waste your time with unimportant and irrelevant information. Likewise the matter of the Little-Endians and Big-Endians: "thousands have willingly suffered death rather than break their Eggs at the smaller end" provides just the context you need to understand the point being made without going into the whole history of that particular feature of Lilliputian history.

How much to tell and how much to leave out is a question that must remain at the forefront of your thinking as you write analysis of effect or technique. With practice in both reading good analytical essays and writing essays of your own, you will develop a sense of appropriateness, and eventually achieve a talent for economy, a characteristic your readers will admire. Recall that in Unit 1 you started with purpose followed by technique; here in Unit 5, you may start with technique followed by effect.

PORTAL POINTS FOR ANALYSIS OF EFFECT OR TECHNIQUE:

When writing essays that analyze an author's effect or technique, key points to consider are:

- where do the author's uses of particular literary techniques suggest that the material has a universal rather than a particular meaning;
- how can I relate necessary plot details while still focusing on analysis;
- how can I arrange the material to best illustrate the cumulative effect of the author's literary choices.

To help you write an essay analyzing an effect or technique, examine the following templates. Think of these templates not only as a road map of what direction to take in your writing, but also as a useful vocabulary for this direction.

Templates for Analysis by Effect or Technique

▼ **Introducing a prominent effect or technique**
These templates identify the position your essay will take.

The author's use of _____ helps convey the theme that _____.

The overall mood is _____.

The author's view towards _____ is _____.

▼ **Coupling content and technique**
These templates establish the relationship between the technique and the theme.

The text's humor reveals the narrator's belief that _____.

The motif of _____ complements the conflict of _____.

Characters complement setting in this way:_____ .

The setting triggers these conflicts, because . . .

All of these elements convey a _____ mood, one that also reflects the author's view towards _____.

_____ occurs, as if to suggest that _____.

▼ **Idea-based transitions, or presenting a linear essay**
These templates help you move through your discussion of a particular technique.

And why does the author present _____ in such a way?

And why might the author have chosen to incorporate _____?

On one level, the text suggests _____. Taken symbolically, however, _____.

All of the recurring elements of the text point to this_____.

Indeed, _____ actions reflect something larger:_____,

These templates allow you to consider more than one technique at a time.

The diction and syntax only reveal the character's _____.

The satirical elements are best achieved through the incongruity and distortion.

All elements point to one main focus: the author's target of _____.

Elements X, Y, and *Z* combine to create a _____ effect.

Elements X, Y, and *Z* create a persona who believes _____.

▼ **Making connections between the start and finish of the text**

These templates give your essay some unity.

We are reminded of the opening images of the text....

One considers how this final image parallels the opening imagery, which shows....

Has the narrator truly been influenced by his discoveries?

Has there been any real change from start to finish?

Review these templates frequently, so that you can utilize their forms and content for future analyses of technique.

The Conversation Begins

A standard prompt that encourages an analysis by effect or technique reads:

> **Analyze** how the writer's use of [techniques] depicts a particular literary element.

In this case, you are examining the relationship between the techniques an author uses and their overall effect or depiction of a particular literary element. To help you compose a successful analysis of technique, complete the following steps.

Step 1: *Reading the prompt*

Read the sample prompt that focuses on analysis by effect or technique.

> Following is a passage from the first pages of *The Berlin Stories* by Christopher Isherwood, a collection of stories about the author's temporary residence in Berlin between the two world wars. In these paragraphs the narrator describes his living accommodations and his landlady. Read the passage carefully, noting the details the author uses to describe the boarding house and its previous tenants. Then write an essay in which you show how the descriptive details combine to provide not only the setting but also the narrator's attitude toward his surroundings and his landlady. Do not merely summarize the passage.

Step 2: *Pre-writing*

Discourse Questions The following questions will assist both your reading and writing experience.

1. What literary techniques does the prose employ, and to what effect?

2. Try organizing or "chunking" the text into 4-5 distinct parts. What is the major point or idea of each section? What remarkable feats of language does each section present?

3. What are the most significant literal details?

4. What are the most significant symbolic, or non-literal details?

5. If someone were to ask you what this was about or what was the point of this piece, what would you say?

Step 3: *Reading the text*

As you read this sample prompt and prepare to compose your response, pay attention to the accompanying annotations that monitor how details combine to convey the setting and the narrator's attitude towards his surroundings.

Excerpt from The Berlin Stories

Annotation

The extraordinary smell in this room when the stove is lighted and the window shut; not altogether unpleasant, a mixture of incense and stale buns. The tall tiled stove, gorgeously coloured, like an altar. The washstand like a Gothic shrine. The cupboard is also Gothic,

5 with carved cathedral windows: Bismarck faces the King of Prussia in stained glass. My best chair would do for a bishop's throne. In the corner, three sham mediæval halberds[1] (from a theatrical touring company?) are fastened together to form a hatstand. Frl.[2] Schroeder unscrews the heads of the halberds and polishes them from time to

10 time. They are heavy and sharp enough to kill.

Everything in the room is like that: unnecessarily solid, abnormally heavy and dangerously sharp. Here, at the writing-table, I am confronted by a phalanx of metal objects—a pair of candlesticks shaped like entwined serpents, an ashtray from which emerges the

15 head of a crocodile, a paper-knife copied from a Florentine dagger, a brass dolphin holding on the end of its tail a small broken clock. What becomes of such things? How could they ever be destroyed? They will probably remain intact for thousands of years: people will treasure them in museums. Or perhaps they will merely be melted

20 down for munitions in a war. Every morning, Frl. Schroeder arranges them very carefully in certain unvarying positions: there they stand, like an uncompromising statement of her views of Capital and Society, Religion and Sex.

All day long she goes padding about the large dingy flat. Shape-

25 less but alert, she waddles from room to room, in carpet slippers and a flowered dressing-gown pinned ingeniously together, so that not an inch of petticoat or bodice is to be seen, flicking with her duster, peeping, spying, poking her short pointed nose into the cupboards and luggage of her lodgers. She has dark, bright inquisitive eyes and pretty

30 waved brown hair of which she is proud. She must be about fifty-five years old.

Imagery conveys both holiness and age

Frl. Schroeder resembles the décor in color.

1 halberd—a pole-like weapon
2 Frl.—Fräulein, German for Miss

Long ago, before the War and the Inflation, she used to be comparatively well off. She went to the Baltic for her summer holidays and kept a maid to do the housework. For the last thirty years she has lived here and taken in lodgers. She started doing it because she liked to have company.

"'Lina,' my friends used to say to me, 'however can you? How can you bear to have strange people living in your rooms and spoiling your furniture, especially when you've got the money to be independent?' And I'd always give them the same answer. '*My* lodgers aren't lodgers,' I used to say. 'They're my guests.'

"You see, Herr Issyvoo, in those days I could afford to be very particular about the sort of people who came to live here. I could pick and choose. I only took them really well connected and well educated—proper gentlefolk (like yourself, Herr Issyvoo). I had a Freiherr[3] once, and a Rittmeister[4] and a Professor. They often gave me presents—a bottle of cognac or a box of chocolates or some flowers. And when one of them went away for his holidays he'd always send me a card—from London, it might be, or Paris, or Baden-Baden. Ever such pretty cards I used to get . . ."

> This imagery presents a more fruitful time and is presented with nostalgia.

And now Frl. Schroeder has not even got a room of her own. She has to sleep in the living-room, behind a screen, on a small sofa with broken springs. As in so many of the older Berlin flats, our living-room connects the front part of the house with the back. The lodgers who live in the front have to pass through the living-room on their way to the bathroom, so that Frl. Schroeder is often disturbed during the night. "But I drop off again at once. It doesn't worry me. I'm much too tired." She has to do all the housework herself and it takes up most of her day. "Twenty years ago, if anybody had told me to scrub my own floors, I'd have slapped his face for him. But you get used to it. You get used to anything. Why, I remember the time when I'd have sooner cut off my right hand than empty this chamber[5] ... And now," says Frl. Schroeder, suiting the action to the word, "my goodness! It's no more to me than pouring out a cup of tea!"

> The persona seems more disturbed by the changes than the landlady.

• • •

She is fond of pointing out to me the various marks and stains left by lodgers who have inhabited this room.

"Yes, Herr Issyvoo, I've something to remember each of them by. . . . Look there, on the rug—I've sent it to the cleaners I don't know how often but nothing will get it out—that's where Herr Noeske was sick after his birthday party. What in the world can he have been eating, to make a mess like that? He'd come to Berlin to study, you

---

3 Freiherr—a title of minor German nobility, roughly equivalent to a baron
4 Rittmeister—literally a riding master, a military title similar to captain
5 She is about to say "chamberpot."

know. His parents lived in Brandenburg—a first-class family; oh, I assure you! They had pots of money! His Herr Papa was a surgeon, and of course he wanted his boy to follow in his footsteps. . . . What a charming young man! 'Herr Noeske,' I used to say to him, 'excuse me, but you must really work harder, you with all your brains! Think of your Herr Papa and your Frau Mama; it isn't fair to them to waste their good money like that. Why, if you were to drop it in the Spree it would be better. At least it would make a splash!' I was like a mother to him. And always, when he'd got himself into some scrape—he was terribly thoughtless—he'd come straight to me: 'Schroederschen,' he used to say, 'please don't be angry with me. . . . We were playing cards last night and I lost the whole of this month's allowance. I daren't tell Father. . . .' And then he'd look at me with those great big eyes of his. I knew exactly what he was after, the scamp! But I hadn't the heart to refuse. So I'd sit down and write a letter to his Frau Mama and beg her to forgive him just that once and send some more money. And she always would. . . . Of course, as a woman, I knew how to appeal to a mother's feelings, although I've never had any children of my own. . . . What are you smiling at, Herr Issyvoo? Well, well! Mistakes will happen, you know."

"And that's where the Herr Rittmeister always upset his coffee over the wall-paper. he used to sit there on the couch with his fiancée. 'Herr Rittmeister,' I used to say to him, 'do please drink your coffee at the table. If you'll excuse my saying so, there's plenty of time for the other thing afterwards. . . .' But no, he always would sit on the couch. And then, sure enough, when he began to get a bit excited in his feelings, over went the coffee-cups. . . . Such a handsome gentleman! His Frau Mama and his sister came to visit us sometimes. They liked coming up to Berlin. 'Fräulein Schroeder,' they used to tell me, 'you don't know how lucky you are to be living here, right in the middle of things. We're only country cousins—we envy you! And now tell us all the latest Court scandals!' Of course, they were only joking. They had the sweetest little house, not far from Halberstadt, in the Harz. They used to show me pictures of it. A perfect dream!"

"You see those ink-stains on the carpet? That's where Herr Professor Koch used to shake his fountain-pen. I told him of it a hundred times. In the end, I even laid sheets of blotting-paper on the floor around his chair. He was so absent-minded. . . . Such a dear old gentleman! And so simple. I was very fond of him. If I mended a shirt for him or darned his socks, he'd thank me with the tears in his eyes. He liked a bit of fun, too. Sometimes, when he heard me coming, he'd turn out the light and hide behind the door; and then he'd roar like a lion to frighten. Just like a child. . . ."

This anecdote may symbolize the overall waste of the German country during the wars.

This anecdote poses a contrast from the earlier orderliness and rigidity, and there is a wistfulness in the description.

Frl. Schroeder can go on like this, without repeating herself, by the hour. When I have been listening to her for some time, I find myself relapsing into a curious trance-like state of depression. I begin to feel profoundly unhappy. Where are all those lodgers now? Where, in another ten years, shall I be, myself? Certainly not here. How many seas and frontiers shall I have to cross to reach that distant day; how far shall I have to travel, on foot, on horseback, by car, push-bike, aeroplane, steamer, train, lift, moving-staircase and tram? How much money shall I need for that enormous journey? How much food must I gradually, wearily consume on my way? How many pairs of shoes shall I wear out? How many thousands of cigarettes shall I smoke? How many cups of tea shall I drink and how many glasses of beer? What an awful tasteless prospect! And yet—to have to die. . . . A sudden vague pang of apprehension grips my bowels and I have to excuse myself in order to go to the lavatory.

The speaker recognizes that this is a time that is long gone.

Christopher Isherwood

Complete the graphic organizer as a way of synthesizing information:

Examples of language	Influence on literary element #1 (i.e., setting)	Influence on literary element #1 (i.e., character)	Influence on literary element #1 (i.e., mood)
Denotative or literal language			
Connotative or symbolic language			

Step 4: *Speaking first, then listening in*

You Try It Write the first 250 words of your response in your own notebook, in a graphic organizer like the one below, and underline those sentences that make active use of the templates.

In the margin on the right, identify the templates that you have used.

Original response to Christopher Isherwood prompt: 1st 250 words	Identification of templates used

Listening In Now, listen in to the sample response. Read the sample response and templates used. Observe how your use of templates compares with those in the sample response.

Sample response to Christopher Isherwood prompt

      If people are products of their environment, then Frl. Schroeder of Christopher Isherwood's *The Berlin Stories* presents the embodiment of a Germany that has seen better days, but still proudly holds on to its heritage. On the surface the setting appears dark, heavy, overly ornamental, burdened by tradition. Yet beneath this "museum" is a vibrancy that—when offered the chance—comes to life through the voice of this museum's curator, Frl. Schroeder.

      The abundance of dark, heavy imagery conveys an oppressive environment. The "Gothic shrine" represents a yearning for days gone by, a reverence for the past based more on tradition than on logical beliefs. The narrator's descriptions of "medieval halberds" with potentially deadly qualities, candlesticks with serpent-like features, and ornamentation in his boarding room acting like a phalanx all communicate a militant, defensive posture. Even the "small broken clock" reinforces a land lost in time. These objects occupy the boarding room, every day cleaned and reporting for duty by the constant Frl. Schroeder, who reverently prepares these objects for a world that may have passed them by. Ironically, their practical use would be to melt them down for war, so even a contemporary use of these objects has a militant quality.

      On one level, Frl. Schroeder herself complements this rigidity, as she is described as "intact" as these objects; she is as duty-bound as they come. Beneath this veneer lies a more animated life, one whose visage and stories come to life for the boarders. Her "flowered dress-

Identification of templates

Introducing overall effect (mood)

Combining technique and content

Synthesizing elements to produce a greater effect

ing gown" and "dark, bright inquisitive eyes" reflect this spark, as does her love of retelling the stories of yesteryear's boarders.

Indeed, the landlady's own stories reflect her own change in social status, for which the narrator expresses clear admiration. By her own admission, Frl. Schroeder would at one point never deign to clean a bathroom, accustomed as she was to more wealth and privilege. But today she does this menial labor as if it were "pouring out a cup of tea"; her stories describe stains—of ink, coffee, vomit, wasted opportunities—but she feels no real remorse or bitterness, for she has come to terms with her place in life.

Her stories, in fact, are a microcosm of her own world. The youthful Herr Noeske wasted his parents' money on a card game and debauchery; she was there to mollify the awkward situation with his parents. The Herr Rittmeister's excitement inevitably produced coffee stains on her wall; his good looks and cosmopolitan connections brought life (though a bit dirty) into the landlady's home. Her fondness for Professor Koch reflected her admiration for his intellect; her mending of his shirts—or cleaning of the stains—reflected her willingness to help "clean" the dirt of everyday living. The landlady lived vicariously through these other people.

The narrator's own journey only begins at the landlady's home, for to label it a museum would suggest a type of ending point, a receptacle for people, artifacts, or stories that no longer exist. But the landlady's home—through the voice of Frl. Schroeder—remains animated in her memories. How ironic that the narrator's incessant consumption of beer, cigarettes, and tea remains "tasteless," as if to suggest that he has entered a world that is past his powers of "apprehension." He cannot grasp this, and in one final symbolic gesture, he must release his bowels, as if to suggest that this release will somehow liberate him to experience the past more fully.

This moment also reveals the setting's influence on the narrator, for his initial observation focused on the age and intractability of his boarding room. Yet his final reflections comment on the impossibility of attaining his goals, no matter how modern or efficient his method of travel becomes: an aeroplane, steamer, train, etc. For he can no more easily achieve what he's looking for through modern convenience than the landlady can recapture her past. They are both types of ornaments adorning the room, a phalanx against the irrevocable onslaught of change and decay.

Idea-based transition

Synthesizing elements for a greater effect

Connecting technique and content

Making connections between the start and the finish

Commentary

This kind of question is a common one, calling for attention to detail and application of observed details to the overall sense of the passage's meaning. The templates suggested in this portal will help you to make good use of the details you observe in a passage given for analysis.

One template that combines technique and content is:

> All of these elements convey a ____ mood, one that also reflects the author's view towards _____.

In its actual use in this essay, the sentence emerges as:

> The abundance of dark, heavy imagery conveys an oppressive environment.

The descriptive phrase "an oppressive environment" provides the "what did the author do" portion of the statement. To create this environment or view, the author has used the "dark, heavy imagery" that is about to be detailed in the next few sentences of this paragraph. This is a fairly traditional paragraph, then, but it has the virtue of combining the observation about the imagery with the purpose of that imagery. The template makes that combination possible.

The same effect results in a sentence in the last paragraph before the end of the essay.

> How ironic that the narrator's incessant consumption of beer, cigarettes, and tea remains "tasteless," as if to suggest that he has entered a world that is past his powers of "apprehension."

Once again, the template provides a means for combining the explanation of what the technique is ("incessant consumption of beer, cigarettes, and tea remains 'tasteless,'" with its meaning ("as if to suggest that he has entered a world that is past his powers of "apprehension").

 Wrapping Up the Portal These templates not only remind you that you have a double task in analyzing prose—to explain both what the author accomplished and how the author accomplished it—but they also assist you in getting that double job done.

Portal 3

**Finding the
Portal**

**The Reading
Experience**

**The Writing
Experience**

Analysis of Theme or Purpose

While nonfiction is about facts, fiction is also about truth, and often the analysis of prose reveals a social purpose. Perhaps that intent of the prose writer finds a close relative in the role of creative nonfiction or memoir, in which the writer deliberately fictionalizes key elements in order to present his or her purpose. And in the process of creating fiction, the author expects of the readers a new array of skills with which to access text.

When you read prose fiction you pay attention to many elements at once. Indeed, we consider the ability to process multiple elements of the literature to be a sign of reading maturity. You may have had the experience of reading a book for a second time and marveling over how much more there seemed to be in the book the second time through. Of course, everything was there the first time, but you contributed more the second time, either because you were no longer trying to keep plot complications straight in your mind, or because you had decided to focus on some other element, or because you simply gave the reading a different kind of attention the second time than you did the first. (The same is true when you see a good film or listen to music. Repeated exposure brings additional rewards. That is one way we determine that a work of art has merit. What they have to offer is not depleted in one visit.)

For most works of literature, the ultimate prize is an awareness of the **theme**, so an analysis that focuses on that feature of the novel, story, or play will likely make the work more meaningful not only to the reader of your essay, but more important, to you.

The writer's message remains couched among myriad details that he or she has placed with a specific purpose in mind. Consider, for example, the personification of the Mississippi River in *The Adventures of Huckleberry Finn* as a complement to Twain's diatribe against the evils of slavery; Faulkner's competing motifs of rain and heat in *As I Lay Dying* to illustrate the dangers of dysfunctional families; Jamaica Kincaid's subtle but effective incorporation of European imagery to reflect the hegemony of social oppression in her essay "Autobiography of a Dress."

The opportunity to analyze purpose in prose presents itself in many forms: social satire, philosophical treatise, apology, aesthetic appreciation, and political diatribe. At the heart of purposeful prose lies an author's interest in communicating a statement of truth with a timeless quality. Rather than making a speech on the corner soapbox, for example, the writer couches his or her message in ways that appeal as much to an audience's imagination as to its inspiration.

When you analyze for purpose, your approach towards the prose is conceptual. Yes, the narrative follows a linear path, and yes, you monitor shifts in tone, imagery, diction, and other features of the text. But your task is to consider a writer's exigence—the real-life purpose behind this fictional creation—and to see how that purpose successfully manifests itself through fiction.

More traditional approaches towards prose analysis will ask you to synthesize various components of the text into a larger whole. Unlike the work of rhetorical analysis, in which you determine an author's *purpose* or *message*, prose analysis of fiction explores a *theme*, a universal, timeless message.

PORTAL POINTS FOR ANALYSIS OF THEME OR PURPOSE:

When writing essays that analyze a passage's theme or purpose, key points to consider are:

- what can we learn about the theme or purpose of the story;
- is there a pivotal moment that best illuminates the purpose;
- who or what may disagree with the theme or purpose.

To help you write an essay analyzing theme or purpose, examine the following templates. Think of these templates not only as a road map of what direction to take in your writing, but also as a useful vocabulary for this direction.

Templates for Analysis of Theme or Purpose

▼ Templates for analysis of theme or purpose
These templates introduce the main idea of your essay.

The purpose of this text is to show the author's belief that ____.

The theme of the text is that ____.

▼ Dealing with plot development
These templates relate the events of the story into your discussion.

If ____ is the case, then so must ____.

If the depiction of ____ means ____, then it follows that the presentation of ____ means ____.

Opposite ____ exists ____, which suggests a new look at the topic:

Yes, ____ does occur; but later the author presents ____.

▼ The rhetorical question to introduce authorial intent
These templates use questions to introduce discussion points.

Can ____ really be the case? Perhaps, but _____.

Why would character *X* do this?

Why did the author choose *not* to present *X*?

Why did the author present *X*?

▼ Evaluating competing truths
These templates acknowledge and introduce a work's complexity.

On one level we are led to believe this. But _____ can also be true when one considers ____.

Consider how these two messages compare or contrast:_____.

Both messages present validity, but for different audiences.

To select one theme as the "right" one would limit our comprehension of _____.

▼ Literary technique to support message
These templates introduce various literary devices into your discussion.

On a metaphoric level, . . .

On a symbolic level, . . .

The setting complements the message by the use of _____.

Such a message is reinforced by a ____ mood.

The characters are merely mouthpieces for the author's belief that _____.

Review these templates frequently, so that you can utilize their forms and content for future analyses of theme or purpose.

The Conversation Begins

A standard prompt that encourages an analysis by effect or technique reads:

> **Analyze** how the writer's use of [techniques] communicates the author's purpose.

In this case, you are examining the relationship between the techniques an author uses and his or her larger concern or argument. To help you write a successful essay analyzing an author's theme or purpose, complete the following steps.

Step 1: *Reading the prompt*

Read the following prompt and accompanying annotation.

> The following excerpt from Oscar Wilde's *The Picture of Dorian Gray* (1890) features a conversation in which two friends theorize about some of their values. Read the excerpt carefully, paying special attention to the dialogue. Then write an essay in which you explain the differences in the two men's philosophies. Avoid summarizing the conversation.

Step 2: *Pre-writing*

Discourse Questions The following questions will assist both your reading and writing experience.

1. What are the central messages or themes stated?

2. Who or what is the antagonist? What makes this element the antagonist?

3. Does the author reflect a bias towards any character? If so, why?

4. How might a literary element symbolize a truthful element?

5. What is the author's attitude towards his or her topic?

6. Where do you notice a shift or evolution of the message?

7. Where does the fiction take on a rhetorical quality?

Step 3: *Reading the text*

As you read this sample prompt and prepare to compose your response, pay attention to the accompanying annotations that examine the author's purpose.

Excerpt from The Picture of Dorian Gray

From the corner of the divan of Persian saddle-bags on which he was lying, smoking, as was his custom, innumerable cigarettes, Lord Henry Wotton could just catch the gleam of the honey-sweet and honey-coloured blossoms of a laburnum, whose tremulous branches
5 seemed hardly able to bear the burden of a beauty so flamelike as theirs; and now and then the fantastic shadows of birds in flight flitted across the long tussore-silk curtains that were stretched in front of the huge window, producing a kind of momentary Japanese effect, and making him think of those pallid, jade-faced painters of Tokyo
10 who, through the medium of an art that is necessarily immobile, seek to convey the sense of swiftness and motion. The sullen murmur of the bees shouldering their way through the long unmown grass, or circling with monotonous insistence round the dusty gilt horns of the straggling woodbine, seemed to make the stillness more oppressive. The
15 dim roar of London was like the bourdon note of a distant organ.

Despite the birds, there is a heaviness, a buzzing, an oppressiveness here.

In the centre of the room, clamped to an upright easel, stood the full-length portrait of a young man of extraordinary personal beauty, and in front of it, some little distance away, was sitting the artist himself, Basil Hallward, whose sudden disappearance some years ago
20 caused, at the time, such public excitement and gave rise to so many strange conjectures.

As the painter looked at the gracious and comely form he had so skilfully mirrored in his art, a smile of pleasure passed across his face, and seemed about to linger there. But he suddenly started up, and
25 closing his eyes, placed his fingers upon the lids, as though he sought to imprison within his brain some curious dream from which he feared he might awake.

Possibly foreshadowing the artist's philosophy—a type of escape

"It is your best work, Basil, the best thing you have ever done," said Lord Henry languidly. "You must certainly send it next year to the
30 Grosvenor. The Academy is too large and too vulgar. Whenever I have gone there, there have been either so many people that I have not been able to see the pictures, which was dreadful, or so many pictures that I have not been able to see the people, which was worse. The Grosvenor is really the only place."
35 "I don't think I shall send it anywhere," he answered, tossing his

head back in that odd way that used to make his friends laugh at him at Oxford. "No, I won't send it anywhere."

Lord Henry elevated his eyebrows and looked at him in amazement through the thin blue wreaths of smoke that curled up in such fanciful whorls from his heavy, opium-tainted cigarette. "Not send it anywhere? My dear fellow, why? Have you any reason? What odd chaps you painters are! You do anything in the world to gain a reputation. As soon as you have one, you seem to want to throw it away. It is silly of you, for there is only one thing in the world worse than being talked about, and that is not being talked about. A portrait like this would set you far above all the young men in England, and make the old men quite jealous, if old men are ever capable of any emotion."

Lord Henry presents an external appraisal of the great art.

"I know you will laugh at me," he replied, "but I really can't exhibit it. I have put too much of myself into it."

Lord Henry stretched himself out on the divan and laughed.

"Yes, I knew you would; but it is quite true, all the same."

"Too much of yourself in it! Upon my word, Basil, I didn't know you were so vain; and I really can't see any resemblance between you, with your rugged strong face and your coal-black hair, and this young Adonis, who looks as if he was made out of ivory and rose-leaves. Why, my dear Basil, he is a Narcissus, and you—well, of course you have an intellectual expression and all that. But beauty, real beauty, ends where an intellectual expression begins. Intellect is in itself a mode of exaggeration, and destroys the harmony of any face. The moment one sits down to think, one becomes all nose, or all forehead, or something horrid. Look at the successful men in any of the learned professions. How perfectly hideous they are! Except, of course, in the Church. But then in the Church they don't think. A bishop keeps on saying at the age of eighty what he was told to say when he was a boy of eighteen, and as a natural consequence he always looks absolutely delightful. Your mysterious young friend, whose name you have never told me, but whose picture really fascinates me, never thinks. I feel quite sure of that. He is some brainless beautiful creature who should be always here in winter when we have no flowers to look at, and always here in summer when we want something to chill our intelligence. Don't flatter yourself, Basil: you are not in the least like him."

The relationship between intellect and beauty is presented, in the context of how this might influence artistic creation.

"You don't understand me, Harry," answered the artist. "Of course I am not like him. I know that perfectly well. Indeed, I should be sorry to look like him. You shrug your shoulders? I am telling you the truth. There is a fatality about all physical and intellectual distinction, the sort of fatality that seems to dog through history the faltering steps of kings. It is better not to be different from one's fellows. The ugly and the stupid have the best of it in this world. They can sit at their ease and gape at the play. If they know nothing of victory, they are at

Basil Hallward represents a differing view, one that lacks the timelessness of Lord Henry's vision.

80   least spared the knowledge of defeat. They live as we all should live—
      undisturbed, indifferent, and without disquiet. They neither bring
      ruin upon others, nor ever receive it from alien hands. Your rank and
      wealth, Harry; my brains, such as they are--my art, whatever it may be
      worth; Dorian Gray's good looks--we shall all suffer for what the gods
85   have given us, suffer terribly."

   Oscar Wilde

   Now copy and complete the graphic organizer in your notebook prior
   to writing a sample response.

Section of the text	Message	Noteworthy literary elements	Denotative or connotative language
1st			
2nd			
3rd			
4th			

Guided Practice

Step 4: *Speaking first, then listening in.*

You Try It Write the first 250 words of your response in your notebook
using a graphic organizer like the one below, and underline those
sentences that make active use of the templates. In the margin on the
right, identify the templates that you have used.

Original response to the Oscar Wilde prompt: first 250 words	Identification of templates used

Listening In Read the sample response and templates used. Observe how your use of templates compares with those in the sample response.

Sample response to Oscar Wilde prompt

Beyond more immediate conflicts between conformity and individuality, Oscar Wilde's two characters present a larger version of such a dilemma: how artistic expression agrees or disagrees with a prevailing culture. Is it the role of the artist to provoke and extend? Or is it the role of the artist to confirm and satisfy? Wilde's two characters present opposing perspectives on more than just how art is recognized, but also on how art reflects either the artist or the observer.

Set amid the heavy, burdened, almost gilded environment of Basil Hallward's art studio—burdened by droning bees and the distant discord of London—Basil Hallward's creation appears secretive, as if to add to the burdened atmosphere; Wilde writes how Hallward "sought to imprison within his brain some curious dream," as if to suggest that the beauty or fantasy of his creation must somehow remain secret.

Hallward confirms as much as he identifies the "fatality" of distinction. His reference to the "ugly and the stupid" serves as a contrast to the florid, exquisite artistic portrait that he has just made. Hallward seems hypocritical, for why would he create such beauty only to hide it? Or only to praise the exact opposite of what he has developed? Hallward's reference to the distant monarchial rules, coupled with a general desire for hedonism and ennui among the upper classes, suggests that the *public* role of art is more to placate or to satisfy. Hallward states that those less artistic, less individual, less creative "live as we all should live—undisturbed, indifferent, and without disquiet." His criteria suggest inactivity and unwillingness to move the public away from preconceived notions. The role of the portrait is *not* to "bring ruin...nor ever receive it" from others; in other words, artistic creation has a type of military value, where there are winners and losers.

Hallward's internal philosophy is paradoxical, for while he (and others) may "suffer terribly" for the beauty of the art that his subject presents, the artist Hallward still clearly identifies with this his subject: "I have put too much of myself into it," he states, and in so doing, Hallward invokes both the personal and vulnerable nature of the artist. If art is to be effective and meaningful, then it must be connected to the creator's soul, but this relationship itself carries such a risk not only to the artist, but also to the public.

Identification of templates

Introduction of philosophy

Incorporating technique into the larger discussion

The rhetorical question to introduce authorial intent

Extending characters' statements into authorial intent

The if...then relationship as a precursor to truth or theme

Opposite Hallward's contemplative, self-abnegating view of art, Lord Henry promotes and provokes, citing the value of art as the very essence of controversy and growth, in that order. For without dissonance there can be no growth, regardless of the discomfort it may bring to the artist or creation. Small wonder that his cigar is tainted with opium, and his initial request does seem to suggest a more superficial value to art. He cites the value of Hallward's growing reputation as an artist, and that public display is mandatory for the artist's best work.

Using contrast to produce a desired effect

Henry's reasons extend beyond personal gain—unlike Hallward's worry about personal loss—into the realm of the public's notion of intellect. Hallward notes that "beauty ends where an intellectual expression begins," and that the role of art is to be emotionally evocative; the public should not allow its institutions to saddle interpretation with intellect or meaning.

Extending into authorial intent

Hallward's diatribe extends to the church, and he cites the example of a bishop who has espoused the same philosophies for an entire lifetime. Rather, Hallward prefers the "brainless beautiful creature" to the world of the intellect. Does this mean that the role of art is to appeal to our basest instincts? Perhaps, but equally important is that Henry cites the importance of *not* guarding art with one's personal feelings, regardless of whatever critical acclaim or insults are presented. Hallward's allusion to Greek mythology presents two additional layers of interpretation. One, comparing the subject to Adonis invokes the Greek ideals of matching physical beauty with intellectual perfection. Two, the allusion to Narcissus both critiques Basil—and his worry that he has put too much of himself into the subject—and praises Basil, for it is the very narcissism of art that carries its core emotional weight.

Evaluating competing truths

Literary technique to support message

Hallward's disinclination to provide the subject's name again reflects his vulnerability and the need to protect his creation. On a symbolic level, this nameless quality—echoed by Lord Henry—reflects the very mystery of art that Henry so admires, for this eternal uncertainty over the identity of a subject, much less the motivations of the artist in the creation of that subject, allows each interpretation to begin anew, and this is the very vibrancy, even necessity, of art in the public domain.

Writing symbolically

Does Henry's philosophy carry inevitable risk of destruction or buffoonery? Certainly, but if Hallward represents an overly intellectual, rational approach to the subject, then he is balanced (or opposed) by Henry's more emotional appeals. Ironically, when Henry says to Basil, "Don't flatter yourself, Basil: you are not in the least like him," he is insulting Basil on two levels. On the more immediate or literal level, he is telling Basil that—contrary to Basil's beliefs—he has *not* put

Using the if...then logic

too much of himself into the portrait, and he therefore has an overly narcissistic view of himself. But on a metaphoric level, he is explaining to Basil that how the public perceives art may have very little to do with what its creators initially intended.

Writing symbolically

Commentary

In this sample response, in addition to seeing how the particular tasks of the question receive treatment, you have a chance to see a specific technique at work: the rhetorical question. Rhetorical questions are questions that are asked without expectation of answer, often because the writer already knows the answer or because putting the statement in the form of a question implies that the answer is so obvious that it need not be given.

> Why would character *X* do this?

In our essay, this statement appears as

> Hallward seems hypocritical, for why would he create such beauty only to hide it? Or only to praise the exact opposite of what he has developed?

Here the rhetorical question serves to introduce the analysis of theme that the material implies. It is important to note a very often overlooked truth about rhetorical questions. They can be excellent devices for introducing ideas, raising issues, implying attitudes, and accomplishing any number of other tasks that the writer needs to do. What they cannot do is illustrate anything, and certainly not prove anything. Some readers who do not apply much critical thinking to what they read will be convinced by a well-placed and well-phrased rhetorical question that the writer's point has been made. In reality, nothing of the sort has happened. The only thing the writer has done by using a rhetorical question is to manipulate the reader into thinking about a particular issue in the way the writer wanted.

If the paragraph had not gone on to consider possible responses to the question, the technique would have been a weakness rather than a strength. If you return to the essay and re-read the paragraph in which this sentence appears (the essay's third), you will see that the remainder of the paragraph considers a reply, and settles eventually on a reasonable resolution to the question. This is the way to avoid the misuse of rhetorical questions.

Wrapping Up the Unit You might want to practice the use of rhetorical questions when you write your next sample essay. They are especially useful when writing about themes, because in the hands of a good writer they point clearly to considerations of abstract ideas, and that is what your analysis of theme and purpose will eventually want to address.

The Open-Ended Response

Portal 1

Finding the Portal

The Reading Experience

Literary Argument by Chronology

In an open-ended response, applying a quotation, element, concept, or idea to a literary text produces original argument. The literary text, in turn, presents itself as a vehicle by which you achieve greater understanding of that particular quotation, element, concept, or idea. You must avoid summarizing the literary text as a whole while creating your original argument.

Perhaps the most inviting entry into writing about a complete text—given the responsibility of applying a concept, element, or idea—is a **literary argument by chronology**. By this method, you start at the beginning of the text, and, as your thoughts and words apply themselves to the text, you progress in the order in which the pages appear. Such an approach works well with texts that themselves follow a linear progression. A Shakespeare play, for example, moves in a chronological fashion. Its evolution of character or ideas is central to discovering deeper meaning. Novels like *The Scarlet Letter* or *The Great Gatsby,* though making some use of flashback, are other examples that lend themselves to looking at how the ending of the text differs from the beginning.

The reading experience for the open-ended response is more than the book you've read last, or even the titles you may have read within the past year. Rather, the reading experience represents your sum total of immersion in canonical or critically acclaimed texts, as well as the full scope of skills you bring to this array of literature. In an argument by chronology, various texts lend themselves well to monitoring how key ideas, concepts, or elements develop from start to finish of a text. Your reading of many Shakespeare plays, for example, may convey the ways in which paradox creates both conflict and truth, as seen in *Romeo and Juliet, Measure for Measure,* or *Hamlet*; your reading of Jane Austen cultivates an awareness of the ways in which characters' motivations are contextualized within societal constraints, as seen in *Pride and Prejudice, Emma,* and *Sense and Sensibility.* Or your experience with 20th century American literature—such as novels by Hemingway or Steinbeck—provides a foundation in seeing how individuals overcome the shackles of conformity.

The Writing Experience

Similar to your experiences in creating original argument, writing a response to the open-ended response calls upon reading experiences much farther removed from the moment you sit down to write the exam. As in an original argument, you avail yourself of prior knowledge to formulate an original opinion. As in an argument, you present an original perspective on a text that has already encountered prior arguments, arguments couched in the genre of literary analysis. And as in an argument, you enter into a conversation that presupposes conversance with a given topic. In other words, you present an informed opinion.

But unlike original argument, your writing prevails upon the boundaries of a single text. Unlike original argument, which is more timely, the open-response is more *timeless*, attending to universal themes espoused by classical literature. And, unlike original argument, where attention to two or more sides of an issue reveals complexity, the open response achieves its complexity through nuanced understanding of literary text.

While your writing task will often be defined by the actual prompt, consider that the texts that you choose may also lend themselves to the approach you wish to take in addressing the writing task.

> **PORTAL POINTS FOR LITERARY ARGUMENT BY CHRONOLOGY:**
>
> The keys to writing an effective literary argument by chronology are:
>
> - the focused application of the prompt to a work of literature;
> - the thorough development of ideas with specific details from the chosen work;
> - control over the elements of good composition.

To help you write a literary argument by chronology, examine the following templates. Think of these templates not only as a road map of what direction to take in your writing, but also as a useful vocabulary for this direction.

Templates For Literary Argument By Chronology

▼ **Introducing the topic**
These templates introduce the element, idea, or quotation to be monitored.

A primary feature of the text is _____.

We are first introduced to _____ when …

The whole point of the story is to show that _____.

▼ **Templates that focus on the beginning of the text**
These templates provide discussion of the beginning of a text.

[author's name]/[title] appears to _____ but actually _____.

The purpose of _____ is to make the author's point that _____.

In [title] the main character, _____, attempts to _____, and by the end accomplishes _____.

_____ is the central conflict of [title].

▼ **Templates that develop comprehension level steps**
These templates provide adequate summary of key points of the text.

It takes a chance remark/moment of _____.

At one point, *X* says/tells _____.

What appears to be *X* is actually *Y*.

When _____ occurs, . . .

The _____ continues as . . .

▼ **Templates that develop application and analysis level steps**
These templates encourage your application of an element to the text.

The conflict between _____ and _____ causes the main character to believe _____, an idea that emerges as a central theme of [title].

X is yet another example of _____ as the text develops.

They underscore the theme that _____ .

▼ **Building towards the end of the text**
These templates encourage connections from the end of the text to the beginning.

The text finally identifies the theme that _____ .

Where before *X* did *Y*, now *X* presents _____ .

What is meant to be *X* is actually *Y*.

▼ **Templates that compare or contrast later parts of text with earlier parts of the text**
These templates provide for a chronological movement through the book, without summarizing.

As the text progresses, we see that _____.

The appearance of _____ later on, however, suggests that _____.

Unlike the previous section, where _____ mattered, now we see that _____.

▼ **Words that evaluate**
These words accompany your evaluation in your original argument.

Actually	Even	Yet
What might be	Really	So

▼ **Determining the claim and the writer's position**
These templates demonstrate an understanding of the author's purpose in a work of fiction.

The author's purpose in this novel is _____.

Given that the text argues for _____, the [concept, element, idea, or quotation] becomes more prominent.

The author believes _____ and makes extensive use of _____ to present her point.

Review these templates frequently, so that you can utilize their forms and content for future Literary Arguments by Chronology.

The Conversation Begins

A standard prompt often features these two tasks:

Examine how a novel develops a particular effect, and **explain** the purpose of that effect.

To accomplish these tasks, complete the following steps.

Step 1: *Recalling the Text*

Prior to writing an argument, make certain that you understand the claim and then compile a significant body of evidence.

Authors sometimes use humor to make the most serious observations about the world around them. Choose a novel or play that uses humor for that purpose. Explain how the author creates humor, and what is the serious purpose behind the author's use of humor in that work. Choose one of these titles, or another of comparable literary merit. Do not merely summarize the plot.

Amis, *Lucky Jim*
Chase, *Harvey*
Díaz, *The Brief Wondrous Life of Oscar Wao*
Dickens, *Bleak House*
Doctorow, *Ragtime*
Fielding, *Tom Jones*
Heller, *Catch-22*
Huxley, *Brave New World*
Irving, *A Prayer for Owen Meany*
Kesey, *One Flew Over the Cuckoo's Nest*
Lewis, *Babbitt*
O'Connor, *Wise Blood*
Shakespeare, *Twelfth Night*
Toole, *A Confederacy of Dunces*
Vonnegut, *Slaughterhouse-Five*
Wright, *Native Son*

Step 2: Pre-writing

Discourse Questions Prior to answering this prompt, respond to the following questions to prepare your essay:

1. What does this question ask me to do, specifically?

2. How do I know if I am "treading water," or staying in the same place in my response?

3. What features of those works apply best to the topic I am assigned to write on? To help you, fill in the graphic organizer like the one below.

Literary Feature	Thematic Implications

4. What broader, more thematic points do I want to make about this topic?

5. How can I progress through the novel chronologically without summarizing?

6. What is my thesis?

As an example for this and the following steps, let's consider Mary Chase's play *Harvey*. There are a lot of funny characters and moments in the play, and you certainly cannot include everything you might know in your essay. So the third pre-writing question becomes a very important one.

Step 3: *Writing and integrating templates*

Listening In Let's listen to how one voice may use the templates in a sample argument by chronology.

Sample response to humor prompt

Identification of templates

In Mary Chase's play *Harvey* we are consistently amused by the characters and behavior of Elwood P. Dowd, his sister Veta Louise, and his niece Myrtle Mae, especially when they are concerned with Elwood's imaginary friend, the six-foot invisible rabbit Harvey. Also providing humor in the play is Dr. Chumley, the founder and director of Chumley's Rest, the psychiatric hospital to which Veta Louise wants to commit her brother so that he will cease to be an embarrassment to her as she conducts her social life and tries to find a husband for Myrtle Mae. The humor is provided by the characters' funny responses to their situation, the plot twists, and the unexpected behaviors of these and other persons of the play, yet behind this humor we can see the author's most serious purpose, to show that kindness and generosity are better approaches to solving life's problems than selfishness, greed, and deceit.

These two templates introduce the topic at a comprehension level.

This introduces the deeper purpose.

Commentary

Notice how key words in this paragraph acknowledge the prompt's emphasis on humor: "constantly amused," " providing humor," "funny responses." The paragraph also responds to the prompt's instruction to explain what serious purpose the author has achieved through the use of humor.

Note, too, how the words highlighted above fall under the templates which identify the main topic:

A primary feature of the text is _____.

We are first introduced to _____ when …

The opening scene of the play takes place as Veta Louise is hosting a party whose purpose is to introduce her daughter, Myrtle Mae, to society, in the hopes that one of her guests will have a son or a nephew who will someday become Myrtle Mae's husband. As basically kind and harmless as Veta Louise and Myrtle Mae are, they are actually critical of the clothing and behavior of their guests. As they are standing in the hallway outside the room where the guests have gathered, they make snide remarks about the appearance and behavior of the women inside the room. Their most critical remarks, however, are reserved for Elwood, Veta Louise's brother, who is a source of embarrassment

Evaluation

Development of an idea

to them, and whose presence at the party they are sure will make the afternoon a disaster. Myrtle Mae calls her uncle "the biggest screwball in town," and in fact, Veta has arranged for Elwood to be away that afternoon precisely so that her friends would not have a chance to meet him. One guest, Mrs. Ethel Chauvenet, however, speaks favorably about Elwood. She says that seeing him was the main reason she came to the party. And when Elwood arrives, he is exceedingly polite and charming to her. The discrepancy between the portrait of Elwood provided by his relatives and the character revealed by his behavior is an early source of humor in the play. The result of that humor is that we see Elwood's family as flawed by their excessive concern over how his eccentric behavior will affect their social aspirations. From the beginning we viewers are allowed to realize that there is something real and meaningful behind the humor.

Comparison with earlier parts of text

Comparison with earlier parts of text

Commentary

As the essay develops, the writer looks at how the humor is created, moving from a more critical element to a humorous element. The templates used include:

> As the text progresses, we see that _____.

> The appearance of _____ later on, however, suggests that _____.

As the use of the templates above suggests, the writer employs a combination of analysis—by comparing earlier and later parts of the text—with evaluation—in this case, rendering a judgment on the true meaning of Veta's remarks.

It is crucial to remember that, in a chronological response, you are *evaluating* the events of the plot as you recount them. Think of this approach as a "Director's Commentary," similar to those found on today's DVDs, where you can replay the movie and hear what the movie director had in mind when he or she made a particular shot. It is the same principle in the chronological approach. Scene by scene, you will note how characters' words and actions develop the play's theme.

For this essay on *Harvey*, the thesis suggests that the essay will demonstrate that, even though funny things happen in the play, these funny moments all support the play's serious theme about kindness and generosity. Some of those funny moments are explained in the body paragraphs in terms of how they contribute to the play's theme. The remainder of your response *builds* upon the opening discussion. Essays that follow this chronological approach do well to consider an image of a staircase, where each step builds upon the prior one as you move towards a discussion of the text's ending.

Step 4: *Application of templates*

You try it Read the remainder of the sample essay on *Harvey* and determine what the type and purpose of each template is. To assist your work, the templates have been highlighted.

Remainder of the sample response to humor prompt

Identification and Analysis of templates

The humorous tone continues as Veta explains to the psychiatrist at Chumley's Rest, where she wants Elwood to be committed, what is troubling her. She is so unnerved by Elwood's friendship with his invisible rabbit that she can't have guests in the house and lead a normal life. She even admits, but only to the doctor and in strict confidence, that sometimes she sees the rabbit too. That is how bad the situation is in the Dowd home. She must get rid of Elwood. But even though she has gone to the hospital to discuss Elwood's case, the doctor comes to believe that it is Veta Louise who is having the nervous breakdown, and has her brought into the hospital instead of Elwood. This mistaken belief is yet another example of the irony that dominates the play. When the doctor and nurse apologize for thinking that Elwood was the prospective patient, his kindness and affability put them at their ease, so much so that they agree to go out for a drink with him when their shift at the hospital is over. These ironies, in the form of reversal of situation, again are quite funny, but they underscore the theme that Elwood's pleasant and agreeable ways are better than the devious, self-centered behavior that motivated Veta Louise to have him locked up.

But Veta Louise is not a monster, and her selfishness is not of the hateful, evil kind. It is a normal human weakness, and one can understand easily how difficult her life must be with a brother whose behavior is so bizarre that she feels she cannot lead a normal life, and worse, that her daughter will always be ostracized because of her eccentric uncle. It takes a chance remark by a cab driver, who is impatient to get away from Chumley's Rest, to make Veta Louise see that Elwood's eccentricity is really a blessing in disguise. Elwood is about to get an injection that will make him no longer see Harvey, and the cab driver who brought the Dowds to the hospital wants to be paid so that he can leave. He tells Veta Louise that he has driven many people from town to the hospital, and they are always very pleasant. But on the way back to town, after they have been treated at the rest home, they become cranky and difficult, and, in what might be an explicit statement of the play's theme, "perfectly normal human being[s] and you know what bastards they are!" Veta realizes in a flash what the new Elwood will be like, and what her life will be like without Harvey's influence on Elwood, and she stops the injection. What is meant to be a funny remark is actually the most sobering moment in the entire play.

The story of Elwood P. Dowd's family trying to attain an amount of normalcy by ridding Elwood of his friend Harvey appears on the surface to be one of lighthearted humor, but an examination of some of the funnier moments in the play reveals that the playwright, Mary Chase, had serious ideas in mind when she wrote it. By the conclusion of the story the audience has been told that normal people are for the most part pretty objectionable, and we are left to conclude that if Harvey makes Elwood less like a normal person, he can't be all that bad.

Wrapping Up the Portal Notice how the essay builds toward the affirmation of the author's theme. In an argument by chronology, where the temptation to tell the story rather than analyze its meaning is strong, your awareness that you are going to arrive at a thematic statement at the end of your essay will help you avoid that weaker approach.

Finding the Portal

The Reading Experience

The Writing Experience

Argument by Literary Element

Argument by chronology presents an inviting way of accessing a text, especially if we enter the text at the beginning and look at the development of an idea from start to finish.

However, there are *many* ways in which an entire novel can be addressed through the open-ended question. Another common approach is **argument by literary element**. With this approach, you look at how a specific literary element conveys a larger meaning throughout the text.

Given the range of literary elements that occupy important roles in literature, accessing a text by monitoring such elements allows you to monitor (1) how a text develops ideas or themes, and (2) the ways in which this particular element enhances the development of this idea or theme.

Literary elements commonly associated with open-ended questions include, but are not limited to:

symbol	character	setting
point of view	conflict	theme
tone	mood	plot
figurative language		

Focusing on a literary element often contributes to an overall analysis of literature, but remember, an effective literary analysis is also an *argument*. In argument by literary element, you are looking at how best to **expand** the discussion of the element into a larger argument, but you are staying within the boundaries of the text.

Reading fiction or drama with an eye toward an integral element manifests itself through your entire range of experiences in analyzing literature. Perhaps your experiences with Victorian literature over the course of a high school career have produced an ability to understand the relationship between layered syntax and authorial irony, as is often the case with either of the Brontë sisters or Dickens; perhaps your experiences with postmodern texts—some of the most difficult material in the canon—have provided you with greater skill in aligning motifs, as is required in understanding William Faulkner or Toni Morrison; or perhaps your total experiences with understanding symbolism has given you skill in reading a text metaphorically, the expectation behind deeper readings of *The Great Gatsby* or *The Scarlet Letter*.

Unlike an argument by chronology, argument by literary element invites more of a crisscross approach towards text, whereby you are encouraged to trace the presentation of an element in the text, not so much in the way in which the element appears, but rather in the way this element serves the larger task at hand.

A standard prompt, for example, may ask:

> Determine how an author's use of [literary element X] contributes to the overall theme or purpose.

One way of exploring an option outside of a chronological manner is to consider the singular and cumulative effect of an element, as seen in the following graphic organizer:

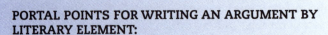

| Recurrence of element | Immediate effect |
| Cumulative effect | Effect on theme or purpose |

The completion of this graphic organizer depends upon your ability to see the difference between *immediate* effects and *cumulative* effects; in other words, the more distant (and cumulative) impact addresses more abstract, conceptual ideas, such as theme or purpose.

Similar to using effective evidence in the argument chapter, the argument by element asks for a *range* of examples, which blend both immediate and distant cases.

PORTAL POINTS FOR WRITING AN ARGUMENT BY LITERARY ELEMENT:

Key points to remember in writing the argument by literary element are:

- the organization is driven less by chronology and more by the cumulative effect of a particular literary element;
- what drives your essay is first the theme or position, with the literary element as the main vehicle in analyzing authorial technique;
- like a position, idea, or theme, the analysis of a literary element can feature shifts or evolution.

To help you write an argument by literary argument, examine the following templates. Think of these templates not only as a road map of what direction to take in your writing, but also as a useful vocabulary for this direction.

Templates for Argument by Literary Element

▼ **Introducing the claim, theme, and/or the writer's position**
These templates help you to begin identifying the major focus of the literary work.

The major purpose/theme/focus of the text is that _____.

The author's ability to communicate ____ is best seen by his statements about _____.

The text states the author's belief that _____.

▼ **Templates that introduce a literary element**
These templates introduce a primary role or location of a literary element.

The _____ reveals the importance of _____.

The novel's main theme, _____, is best represented by the element _____.

_____ reinforces the author's message that _____.

▼ **Templates that pose initial reasoning**
These templates present an initial analysis of the ways in which an element is used.

At first glance, _____ appears to suggest _____.

What is the real reason that _____ exists?

Beyond the effect that *literary element X* has on _____, the real impact of the *literary element X* is _____.

▼ **Expanding upon initial reasoning**
These templates encourage a more expansive approach towards cumulative effects of a literary element.

But what does _____ mean?

By doing _____, the text develops the theme of _____.

A second look at this element reveals something more.

▼ **Aligning technique and authorial intent**
These templates combine what's being said with how it's being said.

The author's purpose is to _____.

By providing *literary element x* at this point, the author conveys _____.

The reasons that the author chooses to do _____ are _____ and _____.

▼ **Templates that equate literary analysis and argument**
These templates combine analysis of literature with presentation of argument.

The real reason that _____ occurs is _____.

Why have _____? Because _____.

Parallels exist when _____.

If indeed the _____, then _____.

▼ **Words that reveal writer's evaluation**
These words convey judgment, an integral aspect of any argument.

Confirmation

Clearly	Successfully	Effectively	Illuminates
Reveals	Similarly	Ultimately	

Speculation

Curiously	Perhaps

Refutation

Fails	Ignores	But

Review these templates frequently, so that you can utilize their forms and content for future Arguments by Literary Element.

The Conversation Begins

A standard prompt often features the following task:

Examine how a novel develops a particular theme or message through the purposeful use of a literary element.

To accomplish this task, complete the following steps.

Step 1: *Recalling the Text*

Prior to writing an argument, make certain that you understand the prompt and then compile a significant body of evidence.

> In literature, as in life, what matters most is often subject to debate. While texts tend to build towards climactic moments, other conflicts or decisions, which seem at first to be less significant, may lead to unexpectedly important results. Choose a novel or play in which a seemingly minor decision presents profound consequences, and explain how that decision and its consequences contribute to the author's overall themes. Do not merely summarize the literature.
>
> Brontë, *Jane Eyre*
> Dickens, *A Tale of Two Cities*
> Ellison, *Invisible Man*
> Faulkner, *As I Lay Dying*
> Fitzgerald, *The Great Gatsby*
> Flaubert, *Madame Bovary*
> Golding, *Lord of the Flies*
> Hansberry, *A Raisin in the Sun*
> Hardy, *Tess of the D'Urbervilles*
> Maugham, *The Razor's Edge*
> Miller, *The Crucible*
> O'Brien, *The Things They Carried*
> Orwell, *1984*
> Shakespeare, *Hamlet*
> Shakespeare, *Romeo and Juliet*
> Steinbeck, *The Grapes of Wrath*

**Guided
Practice**

Step 2: Pre-writing

Discourse Questions To help plan your essay, answer the following questions.

1. What does the novel reveal about this specific literary element?

2. In what way(s) does this element serve a literal purpose? A figurative purpose?

3. Where in the novel do we see the element serving this purpose?

4. When, if ever, does the novel provide examples that fail to support my position?

5. Where does the novel present parallel examples to broaden my understanding of text?

Complete the graphic organizers below to assist you in your planning for the essay.

Recurrence of element	Immediate effect
Cumulative effect	Effect on theme or purpose

Based upon the information that you recorded in the graphic organizers, complete the following questions.

6. What is my thesis?

7. How will I organize my essay? By chronology? By literary element? By some other method?

Guided Practice

Step 3: *Writing and Integrating Templates*

Listening In Let's listen to how one voice may use the templates in a sample argument.

Sample response to consequences prompt

> Charles Dickens's *A Tale of Two Cities* reveals the importance of minor characters in the outcome of the major characters' stories and the overall plot of the novel. However, these characters serve more than the role of foil to chief protagonists; they reinforce Dickens's message that no matter how small or "minor" a person may be, his or her thoughts, actions, or values are as essential as those who are identified as "major." One character who epitomizes this is Miss Pross, whose decision to accompany Lucie Manette to Paris—to help retrieve Lucie's husband, Charles Darnay, from prison—not only saves the lives of the major characters, but almost singlehandedly puts a damper on the Reign of Terror, and—most significant—reveals the fundamental reason why the Reign of Terror fails.
>
> At first glance, Miss Pross's decision to accompany Lucie to Paris reflects her enduring devotion to her Ladybird. A faithful servant, Miss Pross presents herself as a loyal, dedicated nurse to Lucie. Somewhat overprotective at the start, she feels that there are "hundreds of suitors" who seek Lucie's hand in marriage, and while there are only three, her willingness to protect Lucie—at all costs—begins to rein-

Identification of templates

This template introduces the elements to be discussed.

This template introduces the larger argument.

This template establishes the author's purpose.

This template introduces the purpose of the literary element.

This template connects the literary element to a larger purpose or theme.

force Dickens's larger theme of characters' willingness to sacrifice everything—even one's life—for the greater good.

Commentary

Argument by literary element compels you to determine a thematic purpose from the beginning of the essay. Similar to your work with rhetorical analysis or argument, you need to have an awareness of what is at stake. Here, the actions of a minor character do more than cause a ripple effect; they also communicate the importance of equal dignity within all humankind, irrespective of wealth or stature. Thus, the introduction embeds the templates within a discussion of this theme, as seen here:

> Charles Dickens's *A Tale of Two Cities* reveals the importance of minor characters in the outcome of the major characters' stories and the overall plot of the novel. But these characters serve more than the role of foil to chief protagonists; they reinforce Dickens's message that no matter how small or "minor" a person may be, his or her thoughts, actions, or values are as essential as those who are identified as "major."

The above relies on these two templates:

> The _____ reveals the importance of _____.

> The novel's main theme, _____, is best represented by the element _____.

Additionally, the templates provide an avenue to present the larger claim, thereby connecting the literary element (in this case, plot) to a greater concern. The template used is:

> The text states the author's belief that _____.

And the creative manifestation of this template is:

> . . . but almost singlehandedly puts a damper on the Reign of Terror, and—most significant—reveals the fundamental reason why the Reign of Terror fails.

The next sentence provides a preliminary analysis, noting an initial claim about an action. The template used is:

> At first glance, _____ appears to suggest _____.

And the actual language:

> At first glance, Miss Pross's decision to accompany Lucie to Paris reflects her enduring devotion to her Ladybird.

But the next sentence begins to observe a more cumulative effect, using this template:

> By doing _____, the text develops the theme of _____ ,

with the actual sentence as:

> . . . to reinforce Dickens's larger theme of characters' willingness to sacrifice everything—even one's life—

Continue reading in the sample essay on *A Tale of Two Cities*, paying attention to the use of the templates.

Continuation of sample response to Charles Dickens prompt

Identification of templates

But what is the greater good? The novel presents the "best and worst" of times, with characters such as Madame Defarge willing to sacrifice life and limb for the Reign of Terror, as opposed to characters like Sydney Carton, who gives his life to preserve the love and endearment of Lucie Manette. Defarge is driven by hate; Carton is driven by love. And both causes begin with injustice. For Defarge, her family has been victimized by years of torment and abuse at the hands of the aristocracy; for Carton, his descent begins with the dog-eat-dog world personified by Stryver's bullying and the suffocating bureaucracy of London's legal establishment.

This template expands the discussion and poses an alternative view.

When Miss Pross happens to be the one who kills Madame Defarge—as opposed to the major character (Sydney) assigned to the "good" side—Dickens juxtaposes the forces of love and hate, with love coming out at the end. It is good fortune that Miss Pross is protecting Lucie in her apartment (though Lucie is already making her escape) when Madame Defarge enters the scene; it is Dickens's testament to love always triumphing over hate that finds Miss Pross embracing Madame Defarge in an act of defense, opposite the latter's devilish desire to pull out her pistol or knife in an execution.

This template equates literary analysis and argument.

Step 4: *Application of templates*

You Try It Read the remainder of the sample essay on *A Tale of Two Cities*. Determine the types and purposes of the templates. To assist your work, the templates have been highlighted.. Pay attention to how the templates point to key elements—characters, images, ideas— in the novel, and how and why they are important.

Remainder of sample response to Charles Dickens prompt

Identification and Analysis of templates

Beyond the plot and saving a character's life, however, Miss Pross's decision to come to Paris reinforces the novel's larger statements about devotion and sacrifice, with attention to the motivation that accompanies such decision. Opposite the relationship between Miss Pross and Lucie is that of The Vengeance and Madame Defarge. In ways similar to Miss Pross's behaviors, The Vengeance looks after Madame Defarge, protects her, and would willingly give her life to ensure that the cause of the Revolution is fulfilled. Ironically, after the gunshot kills Madame Defarge, the next image of The Vengeance is her seeking out "Therese" (Madame Defarge's first name and the only time we hear that appellation), but to no avail. The Vengeance beholds "Darnay's" execution, lonely, dissatisfied, blind to the truth of her mistress's death or of Darnay's escape. Similarly, the next image of Miss Pross after the gunshot is of her going deaf. Dickens's choice of losing her sense of hearing suggests that she, like The Vengeance, must lose something in this pursuit of one's cause, and that even though characters exist in support of other characters, they are not so easily dispensable or two-dimensional that their fates are cut and dried. Also, Miss Pross's naïveté about the sordidness of her brother reveals the same kind of blindness (or deafness) to her family situation as that of the insensitive rage that the unnamed Vengeance carries to the Reign of Terror.

But why have a minor character kill off the major antagonist of the novel? If the novel's symmetry depends upon the even exchange of characters—Darnay for Carton, Lucie for Madame Defarge, Dr. Manette for Monsieur Defarge—then what is it about the presence of this English servant who manages to upset this symmetry by her very presence? Perhaps one answer is to again consider the novel's overall structure, and to explore why Dickens calls this novel a tale of "two" cities, rather than one, since most of the drama occurs in Paris, not in London. Through the first half of the novel, Dickens draws parallels between London and Paris, and he suggests that conditions in one are not appreciably better than in the other. The recursive structure of the novel finds Darnay in prison first in London, then in Paris (twice);

Dr. Manette first in Paris, then in London, then back in Paris, then back in London. Lucie's husband is first British, then French, then both—or neither. Characters in this novel start to represent not just their home cities, but what their cities represent in terms of civility, the rule of law, forgiveness, or sanctuary.

A Tale of Two Cities is a novel about contrasts, and when Miss Pross lands in Paris, the contrast is much clearer than when Darnay lands in Paris. For with the latter (including his wife and daughter), vestiges of the cruel aristocracy exist, and this blurring of identity ultimately lands Darnay in trouble. Is he no better than the British/French spies of Barsad and Cly? According to the French tribunals, he is just as bad and deserves punishment. But Miss Pross is one hundred percent English, and her arrival in the Reign of Terror illuminates how clearly the motivations of the Defarges have strayed from their original course. Then why not have the equally virtuous Mr. Lorry kill off Madame Defarge? Because this is a novel about the power of women, and Dickens maintains the symmetry of female retribution and protection. It is not the Lucie Manettes of the novel who are truly the ideal women, but the Miss Prosses and—in a stranger way—the Madame Defarges, for these women have the capacity for great feeling and willingness to act upon that feeling (as opposed to Lucie, who faints more than any other woman in this text).

The red-haired Miss Pross. Red, the color of life, blood, revenge—but for her and for the good side of the novel—the color of love. Her decision to come to Paris is more than just to carry the luggage or make the bed; it is to show that even though this is a novel about two cities, two women, and two equally passionate sides, there is only one right way to go.

Wrapping Up the Unit The essay that analyzes an element of the writer's craft is a common one in many academic settings—perhaps the one you are most familiar with in your literature classes. The templates here allow you to refine your attention in such an assignment so that you are ultimately focusing on the literature's themes, which should provide you with not only better essay results, but also, and more significantly, greater pleasure in reading these works of literature.